the
wagamama
cookbook

Hugo Arnold

Kyle Cathie Limited

Author Hugo Arnold   **Project editor** Sarah Epton   **Photographer** Deirdre Rooney   **Art direction and design** Vanessa Courtier   **Food stylist** Joss Herd

Props stylist Wei Tang   **Copy editor** Stephanie Horner   **Editorial assistant** Vicki Murrell   **Production** Sha Huxtable and Alice Holloway

First published in Great Britain in 2004 by Kyle Cathie Limited, 122 Arlington Road, London NW1 7HP   general.enquiries@kyle-cathie.com   www.kylecathie.com

ISBN 1 85626 510 2

Text © 2004 wagamama limited

Photography © 2004 wagamama limited

Front cover photograph © Judah Passow

wagamama and positive eating + positive living are registered trademarks of wagamama limited

Hugo Arnold is hereby identified as the author of this work in accordance with Section 77 of the Copyright, Designs and Patents Act 1988

A CIP catalogue record for this book is available from the British Library

Colour separations by Sang Choy, Singapore

Printed and bound in Singapore by Tien Wah Press

All recipes serve 2 people unless otherwise stated

the
wagamama
cookbook

Hugo Arnold

contents

introduction 6

1 the wagamama kitchen 8

2 sauces, dips and dressings 20

3 sides and other small dishes 40

4 chicken 62

5 fish 82

6 meat 116

7 vegetable main dishes 134

8 salads 152

9 desserts 170

10 juices and drinks 184

index and resources 190

introduction

It is 2.30 on a sunny May afternoon and the original wagamama in Streatham Street in London is full. People are still arriving for late lunches, although the queue is not nearly as long as it was an hour ago. On the table next to me are two lovers on their first date. Opposite, a group of eight students sit in animated conversation while along from them an elderly couple hold hands while they drink glasses of raw juice.

My order arrives: *yaki soba* noodles along with a side order of duck *gyoza*, dumplings filled with succulent meat and leeks served with a sweet hoi sin dipping sauce. I hear the students all order by number; five of them go for 77, the others select a 71, a 103 and a 76. These are among the most popular dishes. When the second London wagamama opened in Lexington Street in Soho in 1996, somebody made the mistake of altering a few of the numbers. It caused *great* confusion.

Wagamama first opened its doors to the public in 1992. Since then it has spawned numerous outlets in countries as far apart as Ireland, Holland and Australia and for many — including me — it has redefined the idea of casual eating. The dishes are designed for one-stop eating. I order 'sides' because I'm hungry. Many don't bother and the bill consequently remains remarkably low and very controllable. At wagamama what you order is very plainly what you pay for. There are no hidden extras.

I pick up my chopsticks and start to eat my teppan-fried *yaki soba* noodles. The dish is a treasure trove of ingredients: egg, chicken, prawns, onions, peppers and beansprouts topped with sesame seeds, dried shallots and pickled ginger. The ice-cold Asahi beer hits the back of my throat and I'm feeling very content.

Cooking noodles is easy; this is what lies behind the success of wagamama. A combination of fresh and staple ingredients, delivered swiftly in a range of delicious ways, and presented stylishly. Perfect for the home cook, too, in our time-starved age, which is the reason for this book. Preparation time required for most of the dishes is well inside 15 minutes and most are cooked in under ten, many in less than five. Considering the bulk of the ingredients could be sitting in your cupboard at home and you have the added attraction of convenience.

I finish my *yaki soba* and ask for the bill. My waitress, a young student it turns out, in her final year at college and studying physics, chats away as she keys my request into her hand-held computer. As we talk two more students arrive to join the eight who have already ordered.

In less than 30 seconds their order – given by number, of course – is keyed in and soon they are catching up with their friends over bowls of steaming *ramen* noodles. My bill arrives and in moments I am up on the street again in brilliant sunshine, feeling well fed and refreshed for a very reasonable amount of money.

When wagamama started nothing like it existed. Founder Alan Yau had considerable difficulty persuading anyone that a large basement site behind the British Museum had a chance of surviving, let alone succeeding. Yet he had a vision and determination not only to serve fast, nutritious, Asian-inspired cuisine, but to do so in a stark, restrained and ultramodern environment. Some of the wagamama restaurants undoubtedly are 'softer' than others – there is more use of wood in some of the more recent ones, for example – but they all retain a definite clean, pared-back look that allows customers and staff alike to provide the action and warmth.

Back in my flat the following day I am testing the *cha han* – one of the most popular dishes – for a group of friends. I have been asked by wagamama to write a cookery book explaining the company's approach to cooking noodles and Asian food and how easy this is to achieve at home. For a year I have been immersed in noodle dishes, the workings of a dynamic and growing company, and a group of highly motivated, hard-working people. I am experiencing the way of the noodle.

The recipes in the book are specified for two people on the basis that you can easily scale up if necessary; I am cooking for six. My friends have all offered to bring beer, so my shopping trip was limited to buying chicken and mushrooms. Soon I am chopping and putting ingredients into bowls. By the time I have cooked the rice everything is cleaned down and people arrive. We sit drinking cold beers and chatting. I have to use two frying pans – to see if the recipe will work without a wok – yet I am in the kitchen for less than 10 minutes (the recipe does work).

All the dishes at wagamama are designed to use a set number of ingredients. That is part of the reason why the service is so fast. Wagamama has redefined the expression 'fast food'; taking fresh, nutritious ingredients, cooking them well and delivering them efficiently. For the home cook this means your store cupboard is not huge and shopping is very easy. The whole style of cooking concentrates on intense heat, applied for a short period, allowing the ingredients to shine through and ensuring the cook doesn't spend forever in the kitchen. With these recipes, a sharp knife, a chopping board and a wok you too can cook the wagamama way.

1
the wagamama kitchen

The wagamama restaurant kitchens are organised so that any item on an order goes to one station where it is prepared. The dish is then put up on the 'pass' where it is collected and brought to your table. When you are cooking at home, you are more likely to be preparing a number of dishes together. The key thing to bear in mind is that not much cooking takes place until the last moment. It can seem as if you are chopping and sorting for ages with little to show for your efforts. While this may at first be frustrating, in the end it is part of what makes this cooking so easy.

In the early days of wagamama, much was made of the Japanese management system of *kaizen*, which means continuous improvement or, as chief executive Ian Neill would say, you do something, learn something, do some more things. As with *kaizen* culture, you are using little stages to build the final assembly. Whichever way you choose to explain it, the idea is to chip away and move forward – that way you learn.

Many of the recipes in this book have appeared on the wagamama menu at some time or other. There is nothing complicated or difficult about cooking any of them. We excluded a few of the deep-fried dishes on the grounds that most people don't want to do too much deep frying in their own kitchen and some recipes have been altered slightly to cater for a domestic environment, but in essence they retain the same characteristics as the day they made it through a tasting and on to the menu.

the equipment

There is no need to go out and buy any special equipment. A wok will make things easier – they are not expensive (best bought from Asian stores) – but a large, nonstick frying pan will suffice. Chopsticks will enhance the eating experience, but a fork is fine. *Ramen* bowls are useful if you are going to cook this kind of food frequently. They are quite large, to accommodate the broth, and tend to be made from a material that insulates the heat so you can pick them up. They are, however, quite expensive. It's best to experiment with what you have, initially, and splash out on the kit tomorrow; that way you'll know exactly what you want and why. The one piece of kitchen equipment we did worry about was the teppan, a large flat plate on which the Japanese fry noodles mixed with other ingredients. Yet a heavy-bottomed nonstick frying pan is a perfectly good substitute at home.

Wagamama sells a limited number of items which may be useful for cooking and presenting some of the dishes in this book. These include: *ramen* bowls, *cha han* bowls, wooden *ramen* ladles, sake jugs and cups, *gyoza* trays and *miso* cups and lids. Woks, knives, bowls and chopsticks are all readily found in ethnic food stores.

stir frying – an art or a secret?

While a frying pan can be used in place of a wok, you'll quite quickly discover that the shape and heat dispersal of a wok are unique. And that there is a world of difference between frying and stir frying, which lies in the speed and temperature at which you cook. Tossing food around in a wok may seem a daunting and challenging way of cooking. A degree of technique and skill must be learnt and applied, but it is not as difficult as you may think. Once mastered, it's a dazzling way of impressing your dinner guests and creating some really tasty food to eat.

Wok cooking is about speed. You want to cook the ingredients quickly and preserve as much nutritional value as possible. To do this, you must have heat – and lots of it.

In the wagamama kitchens we have the luxury of purpose-built wok ranges which burn gas in a swirling motion, encouraging the flames to cover the whole base of the wok and not simply fire into one concentrated area. This helps to ensure an even heat distribution over the wok and eliminates any 'cold spots'. The average household does not possess such equipment, although there are now gas hobs which incorporate a central 'wok burner'. Electric, halogen and ceramic hobs are less suited to using a wok than gas hobs, owing to the large amount of movement required during stir frying, which reduces the contact with the heat source. This is where the large nonstick frying pan comes into its own. The larger the better, because the greater the surface area, the better the result.

Before stir frying ensure you have everything you need to hand: all the prepared ingredients, including seasonings, and warmed serving bowls or plates. It is essential to heat the wok thoroughly for 1–2 minutes before adding any oil, otherwise the wok will never get properly hot.

The process of stir frying basically relies on movement. Movement is achieved using either a wok scoop, wooden spoon or spatula, or even chopsticks. You also need to move the wok itself to ensure even heat distribution. The wok can be 'flicked' to move the ingredients around. This is best practised in a cold wok with some raw rice. Tilt the wok lightly away from yourself, gently push forward and then flick your wrist back. This movement causes the ingredients to move to the far edge of the wok and then be 'flicked' back towards you. It is about action, not muscle, and with patience and practice, a basic level of skill can be mastered. The same action can be used with a nonstick frying pan. If you use a scoop, spatula or chopsticks to stir the ingredients, remember to keep them moving. Most stir fries should take no longer than 2–3 minutes to cook.

seasoning a wok   When you buy a wok it needs to be 'seasoned' before its first use. Wash in hot soapy water to remove any packing grease or oil, then basically burn it over a high heat until the whole of the interior changes colour to a deep blue, almost black appearance. Turn off the heat and smear with vegetable oil, covering all the metal, and allow it to soak in. After each use, you should wash and dry the wok thoroughly and rub a little oil over the surface to prevent any rusting.

a wagamama meal

The wagamama menu is designed so that one dish is sufficient for one person, with perhaps a side dish as well if you are hungry. We've constructed the recipes in this book for two people on the basis that two people eating together might like to share a couple of dishes. There are no hard-and-fast rules, however, and if you are catering for four people you may choose to double the quantities of one recipe and leave it at that.

japanese cooking styles   In Japan three cooking styles are traditionally used together in the main part of the meal to ensure variety. There are seven to choose from: deep-fried (*age-mono*), grilled (*yakimono*), sautéed (*itammono*), simmered (*nimono*), steamed (*mushimono*), vinegared (*sunomono*) and dressed salads (*aemono*).

At wagamama we have rather liberally interpreted these styles so they can be incorporated in one dish. This may not be the most authentic Japanese cuisine, but we have never claimed to provide that kind of food.

This is not to say we break the rules with little thought for authenticity. In designing dishes we try to ensure balance and grounding. A monthly tasting looks at every dish being considered and, apart from tasting it, we ask lots of questions, pull it apart and put it back together again. What we are trying to ensure is that not only does a dish taste good, but that it works both for the customer and for the kitchen preparing it. Can we do it consistently well and are there any problems? Only when we are satisfied does it go on the menu.

presentation   Presentation of the meal as well as the table setting is an integral part of Japanese dining. Both aspects are equally important in wagamama and undoubtedly enhance the enjoyment of eating noodles as well as rice dishes.

Sit in a wagamama and your table area has a paper mat and a set of wooden chopsticks specifically for you (both are disposable and produced from sustainable resources). If you find chopsticks difficult, we will give you a fork or spoon, or your server will be happy to explain how to use chopsticks. It is not difficult, but does require a little practice.

All the dishes involving liquid are served in bowls made from lacquer. Lacquer remains cool even when it contains hot liquid, so the bowl can be lifted to drink what clearly cannot be con-veyed to the mouth using chopsticks. All the non-liquid-based dishes are served on plain white plates, with the ingredients cut into bite-sized pieces. So there are two issues here: how to use chopsticks and how to eat noodles.

Using chopsticks enables you to enjoy noodles in the traditional way. This involves slurping. The rationale behind this is the need to incorporate air when you eat, so that you sense the aroma – much more sophisticated than flavour – of the food fully as well as the taste. The soup is slurped and the noodles sucked and the more noise you make, the better.

spiciness   We are often asked by customers if we can spice up dishes for them. Given our streamlined restaurant service, this is not possible, which is why we leave bottles of chilli sauce and soy sauce on the table so customers can help themselves. At home, however, it is possible to increase the chilli heat or spiciness when you are preparing the dish. How much depends on taste and a little experience.

We suggest that you start by following the recipes as specified; that way you know what you are dealing with. If you want more spice, for those recipes that use another sauce, such as *katsu* or *gyoza*, it is a good idea to increase slightly the amount of sauce used. Otherwise, key ingre-dients to pep up the spiciness include: chilli, garlic, ginger, lemongrass and *shichimi* spice. These are by no means the only ones but a 10–20 per cent increase in the amount you add of these ingredients will significantly affect the final spiciness of dishes. Add slowly, and experiment to get the spice kick you enjoy best.

ingredients

Listed below are those ingredients with which you may be rather less familiar than is normally the case in recipe books. Most are obtainable either in large supermarkets or ethnic food stores.

Char siu sauce   A Chinese barbecue sauce that is widely available.

Choi sum   Also known as the Chinese flowering cabbage, it has a sweet, mustardy flavour and is rich in calcium. It will keep for a few days in the fridge.

Chikuwa   Cooked Japanese fishcake, similar to *kamaboko-aka* (see right), sold by the tube in various diameters and lengths. It is available from ethnic food stores. It is mild in flavour and if you have trouble finding it can be omitted without spoiling the overall dish.

Daikon   A mild white radish, also known as *mooli.*

Dashi   A light fish stock made from *konbu*, a seaweed (normally kelp) and dried bonito flakes (*katsuo bushi*) – although dried sardines (*niboshi*) are also used.

Dashi no moto   An instant powdered version of *dashi*, commonly used in domestic kitchens in Japan.

Edamame   Freshly steamed green soya beans. When served in the restaurants they are lightly salted and make an ideal accompaniment to drinks. Hold to your mouth and squeeze the beans from the pod.

Enoki   These mushrooms grow in clumps and have long thin stems and well defined caps. They are delicate in flavour and if cooked correctly retain a crunchy texture.

Fish sauce (*nam pla*)   A thin liquid extracted from salted, fermented fish. It should be light golden brown in colour with a tangy, salty flavour. If it is dark and bitter, discard: fish sauce deteriorates once opened and darkens as it ages.

Gari   Pickled ginger, which was made popular with sushi and is now widely available. It is both sweet and peppery in flavour and varies in strength and in the way it is cut. Fresh ginger root is also much used in Japanese cooking.

Gyoza skins   Small, round, wheat-flour skins sold in Chinese and Japanese food stores and used to make dumplings.

Kamaboko-aka   Japanese fishcakes, traditionally white with a pink outer crust, which can be bought in Oriental stores.

Katsuo bushi   Fermented and dried bonito fish flakes that keep forever, releasing their flavour when soaked in warm water. They are an important ingredient in *dashi* (see left).

Konbu   Kelp seaweed, sold dried (to be reconstituted in water before use) and ready-soaked.

Konnyaku   Otherwise known as yam cake, it is made from the starchy root of the *Amorphallus konjac* plant and smells fishy. It is available from specialist Japanese food stores.

Menma   Pickled bamboo shoots which come in cans and are readily available to buy.

Mikku powder   A Japanese seasoning. You can use salt instead if you can't get *mikku.*

Mirin   Sweetened sake used for cooking.

Miso   A Japanese paste made from fermented soya beans and other ingredients. It comes in a variety of guises, from *Genmai miso*, which is made with brown rice and is chunky and rich, to sweet white *miso* which is light and delicate. Both white and yellow *miso*s are used in this book but it is worth experimenting with others to find one you particularly like. We use the red (*aka*) in the *miso* paste for salmon *ramen* (see page 104).

Miso soup   Made from *dashi* and flavoured with *konbu* seaweed, cabbage and dried shiitake mushrooms. It can also be made with white *miso* paste.

Cooked edamame.

Enoki mushrooms.

Noodles In Japan there are four main types of noodles: *ramen* (Chinese style), *soba* (wholemeal), *udon* (thick white noodles) and *somen* (thin white noodles). Whichever type you use, noodles are always cooked in boiling unsalted water – and lots of it. They are the perfect fast food, offering a nutritionally complete meal in one bowl. A properly composed noodle soup is the quintessence of freshness and natural purity and, like pasta, is a good source of complex carbohydrates which the body can burn most easily to provide energy.

Oyster sauce Made from oysters cooked with soy sauce and seasonings. It is brown and thick like ketchup.

Panko breadcrumbs These have a coarser texture than ordinary breadcrumbs. They make for a much lighter and crunchier coating for deep-fried foods.

Pickled cabbage This has a slightly sour and salty flavour and is used in small quantities and stir fried through a dish. It is sold in cans.

Pickled ginger See *Gari*.

Pickles Almost every vegetable in Japan is pickled or preserved, from *daikon* to aubergine to turnip. This is generally done in salt which retains the vegetables' crunchy texture. Brands vary quite a bit and are widely available. Try several until you find one you particularly like.

Rice Japanese rice, as it is often sold even if grown in America, is short-grained and 'glutinous'. This word is misleading as the rice doesn't actually contain gluten, but two kinds of starch, amylose and amylopectin (sticky rice has around 83 per cent of the latter). The stickiness is important as it is eaten with chopsticks. Contrary to what might be expected, risotto or Spanish rice is closer to the Japanese variety than something like basmati, which is long-grain and not particularly 'glutinous'.

Sake A wine made from rice. Served both warm and cold, it has similarities with dry sherry, which can be used as a substitute in recipes.

Shaoshing **wine** Made from fermented glutinous rice, it is amber in colour, about 15 per cent alcohol by volume and tastes rather sweet, reminiscent of a light sherry, which can be used as a substitute.

Shichimi **or seven-spice pepper** A grainy mixture of chilli pepper, black pepper, dried orange peel, sesame seeds, poppy seeds, slivers of *nori* seaweed and hemp seeds. This is the perfect seasoning for *soba* and *udon* noodle dishes. It is widely available in Oriental stores.

Shiitake A variety of mushroom which, when dried, develops a strong, meaty flavour.

Spicy fish powder A mixture of ground fried fish and *shichimi* spice (see above).

Soy sauce Comes in two versions, light and dark. In general the light is used in cooking and is the one most commonly referred to in the recipes. Dark soy is much saltier and is used to give stronger colour and flavour.

Sweet chilli dipping sauce There are various brands with the sweet/chilli ratio varying. Try them all and find one you like.

Szechuan vegetables Pickled and preserved vegetables, usually sold in cans.

Teriyaki sauce Made from soy sauce, sake, *mirin* and ginger. It is widely available ready made.

Tofu or bean curd Made from soaked, mashed and strained soya beans. There are many varieties available – I recommend you use 'firm' in most of these recipes. It acts like a sponge, absorbing flavours, and is an excellent protein alternative to meat.

Tsuyu **or** *tsuke* **sauce** A traditional Japanese dipping sauce and seasoning. It is basically soy sauce flavoured with seaweed (kelp), dried bonito (a type of fish), sugar and salt. It comes in various strengths.

Wakame A silky textured seaweed often used in soups. It is available from Oriental stores.

White pepper A common seasoning ingredient in Japanese cooking.

Wakame seaweed.

Panko breadcrumbs.

stocks and preparations

Good stock forms the basis of much of the food at wagamama. We use big, specially commissioned containers that hold vast quantities and require taps to drain off the liquid. At home you will be using a saucepan, but the principle remains the same: lots of good ingredients simmered long and slow. A stock will bubble away quite happily without much attention but there are no short-cuts if you want the real thing.

In our busy lives, however, we don't always have time to make stock from scratch. We recognise this, and give you three versions here: a domestic version of our main stock, one that takes about half as long, and a third that can be prepared in minutes. All three are very different, but we are trying to achieve the best possible result within the time available. Two of them make use of chicken stock cubes; these vary quite considerably. You need to experiment to find one that suits you but, as a general rule, delicatessens and health food shops tend to stock the better examples.

Also included here are some of the basic preparations common to a number of recipes. Cooking noodles and rice, for example, and marinating meat. We also briefly cover the cutting of vegetables. Presentation is very important – in each wagamama kitchen there is a manual showing not only what the finished dish should look like, but also how to achieve it.

preparing vegetables and meat
Using chopsticks to eat means each piece of food you pick up has to be bite-sized. That need, balanced by the desire to make each dish visually appealing ensures a lot of attention is paid to the way things are chopped. The wagamama manuals show exactly how a spring onion, a sweet potato and a piece of swordfish should be cut. Perfect presentation may not be quite so critical at home, yet to the eye a spring onion or a carrot cut on the diagonal looks far more attractive than one cut on the square. As a general rule we try to avoid right angles whether slicing meat or vegetables. There is another reason, though: cutting on the diagonal means you expose a greater surface area of the ingredient to heat during stir frying, so it cooks very fast.

Meat is marinated for two reasons: first to help tenderise it and second to impart extra flavour. The tenderising is quite slight, and certainly won't make tough meat tender, but it does help to break down some of the enzymes. Adding flavour is the more important reason. In order to maximise the effects of the marinade, you need to 'massage' it into the meat, which is best done gently by hand. Placing the meat and its marinade in a plastic bag is a good idea.

noodles   The ratio of noodles to liquid is important: in noodle soup dishes, the noodles must not only be suspended in the liquid but also form a platform on which to put the other ingredients. At wagamama we serve 125g (4½oz) of fresh *ramen* noodles in 450ml (16fl oz) of broth. We have adjusted the recipes in this book downwards slightly on the basis that most people's bowls are likely to be smaller than our *ramen* bowls.

In most of the recipes, the noodles are cooked first and then reheated in hot stock to form the finished dish. This is a real bonus which cuts down on last-minute preparation. Noodles, whatever type you buy, are very quick to cook; some only require soaking or fast boiling for 2–3 minutes (refer to the packet instructions of the brand you buy). The cooking technique remains the same: as with pasta, you want plenty of boiling water and a pan big enough to accommodate the noodles and allow them to swirl around. Cooked noodles should still have some bite, or resistance – *al dente*, as the Italians say. Unlike pasta, though, it is usual to cook noodles in unsalted water, the seasoning being adjusted when you make up the final dish.

In order to stop noodles cooking you need to refresh them under lots of cold running water. The cold drained noodles will keep for a few hours in the fridge.

rice   The Japanese use short-grained rice which is cooked so it sticks together slightly – it helps when using chopsticks. You can weigh rice, but volume is often an easier and more accurate method. As a rule, if you chose not to weigh the rice, the ratio of rice to water is 2:3 and you should allow half a cup of rice per person.

Wash the rice in several changes of cold water, swirling it around with your hand to release the starch. Drain in a sieve and leave for 30 minutes. Put in a heavy-bottomed pan, add the correct amount of cold water (so for 2 cups of rice, 3 cups of water), cover with a tight-fitting lid and bring to the boil. Turn the heat down as low as it will go and cook for 10 minutes. Remove from the heat and allow it to sit undisturbed, lid on, for a further 10 minutes. Transfer to a clean container to stop it cooking and serve.

chicken stock (1)

1kg (2lb 4oz) chicken bones • 350g (12oz) pork bones • 1 onion, peeled and chopped • 2 carrots (50g/2oz), chopped • 4 leeks (350g/12oz), sliced • 25g (1oz) fresh ginger root, sliced • 4 Chinese leaves, roughly chopped

Put the meat bones in a large pan, cover with cold water and bring almost to the boil. Turn the heat right down and simmer for 2 hours, skimming off any froth that rises to the surface.

Add the vegetables and another 1 litre (1¾ pints) water, bring almost to the boil again, lower the heat and simmer for a further hour. Remove from the heat and allow to cool. Strain off the liquid, return to the saucepan and simmer for 1 hour to reduce further. Season with the chicken stock seasoning below.

chicken stock seasoning

2 teaspoons salt • 2 teaspoons sugar • small pinch of white pepper • 1 teaspoon *dashi no moto* (see page 14)

chicken stock (2) *when you need to make stock at the same time as cooking*

2 good-quality chicken stock cubes • 500g (1lb 2oz) uncooked chicken thighs or wings • 1 leek, finely chopped • 1 carrot, finely chopped • 1 litre (1¾ pints) water

Combine all the solid ingredients in a pan, add the water and bring almost to boiling point, lower the heat and simmer for 30 minutes. Strain and proceed.

chicken stock (3) *when you want something to eat now!*

2 good-quality chicken stock cubes • 1 leek, finely chopped • 1 carrot, roughly chopped • 2.5cm (1in) piece of fresh ginger root, roughly chopped • 1 litre (1¾ pints) water

Combine all the solid ingredients in a pan, cover with the water, bring to the boil, strain and proceed.

vegetable stock (1)

4 Chinese leaves • 450g (1lb) potatoes, peeled • 2 carrots • 2 tablespoons chopped canned tomatoes • 1 small sweet potato • ½ small butternut squash • 1 white onion • 1 red onion • 1 leek • 3 litres (5 pints) water

Roughly chop all the vegetables and put in a large pan with the water. Bring to the boil, then lower the heat to a gentle simmer and cook, uncovered, for 3 hours. Turn off the heat, allow to cool and strain. Season with the vegetable seasoning below.

vegetable stock seasoning

2 teaspoons salt • 2 teaspoons sugar • pinch of white pepper • small pinch of *mikku* powder (see page 14)

vegetable stock (2) *when you need to make stock at the same time as cooking*

2 good-quality vegetable stock cubes • 2 Chinese leaves • 2 carrots, roughly chopped • few sprigs of flat-leaf parsley • 3 litres (5 pints) water

Place all the ingredients in a large pan and bring to the boil, lower the heat and simmer for 10–15 minutes if time, then strain.

dashi

There are two types of *dashi* fish stock, generally referred to as primary and secondary. An instant, powdered version can be bought in packets known as *dashi no moto* that simply requires water. Making *dashi* from scratch is not difficult and in Japan is considered a real test of a chef. A formal meal will start with a *dashi* broth, the quality of which determines what is likely to follow.

primary dashi

10cm (4in) piece of *konbu* (see page 14) • handful of dried bonito flakes (*katsuo bushi*, see page 14)

Lightly brush the *konbu* with a damp cloth but don't overdo it as much of the flavour lies on the surface. Put the *konbu* with 1 litre (1¾ pints) water in a large pan. Bring to the boil over a medium heat. Remove from the heat, extract the *konbu* and reserve for use in soup. Add the bonito flakes, return the pan to the heat and bring back almost to the boil. Remove from the heat, allow the bonito flakes to sink to the bottom and strain. (If you leave the bonito flakes in the water for too long, they give a bitter flavour.)

secondary dashi

Proceed as above except allow the *konbu* to simmer gently for about 20 minutes before removing it. (This *dashi* is stronger and traditionally used for *miso* and simmering dishes. You can reuse ingredients from primary *dashi*, or use fresh.)

vegetable dashi broth

1 litre (1¾ pints) vegetable stock • scant ½ teaspoon *dashi no moto* (see page 14) • 1 teaspoon salt • 1 teaspoon sugar • pinch of *mikku* powder (see page 14) • pinch of white pepper

Heat the stock and add all the seasonings. This can be used as a broth if you or your guests don't eat fish.

curry oil

2 leeks, trimmed and finely chopped • 2 onions, trimmed and finely chopped • 2.5cm (1in) piece of fresh ginger root, finely chopped • 4 garlic cloves, finely chopped • 225ml (8fl oz) vegetable oil • 1/2 teaspoon dried chilli flakes • 1 bay leaf • 1 cinnamon stick • 2 star anise • 1/2 teaspoon paprika • 1 teaspoon curry powder • 1/2 teaspoon turmeric

Put all the ingredients in a large, heavy-bottomed pan and cook over a low heat for 1 hour. Allow to cool, then strain. Covered, this will keep for a few weeks in the fridge.

miso paste

1/2 glass sake • 40g (1 1/2oz) *aka miso* (red) • 100g (3 1/2oz) *shiro miso* (white) • 1 teaspoon sugar • 2 teaspoons sesame oil • tabasco, to taste • pinch of *shichimi* (see page 15) • generous pinch of *dashi no moto* (see page 14)

Put the sake in a small pan and bring to the boil. Light with a match, remove from the heat and allow to cool down. Combine the remaining ingredients in a bowl, mix well and stir in the sake. This will keep for several days in the fridge.

coconut panko breadcrumbs

110g (4oz) *panko* breadcrumbs (see page 15) • 225g (8oz) desiccated coconut

Combine the breadcrumbs and coconut and store in an airtight container.

shichimi spiced flour

110g (4oz) plain flour • 1 heaped teaspoon *shichimi* (see page 15) • 1 heaped teaspoon sugar • generous pinch of salt

Combine all the ingredients. Store in an airtight container until needed.

2
sauces, dips and dressings

Ramen dishes are traditionally made up of three elements: noodles, a soup base and a prime ingredient of chicken, fish, vegetables or meat. In reality, however, things are not quite that simple and this chapter explains why.

In addition to the three core elements each dish needs added flavour, colour and texture. Sometimes this is achieved with a marinade, sometimes with a sauce, sometimes with a dressing. Most dishes incorporate one of these to give greater depth, an intrigue, another dimension. This is the element that leads you on, the one part of the dish that you cannot quite identify, but which provides interest.

Let's face it, noodles by themselves are quite bland, and so too is rice. And a good stock, while delicious, can become a little tiresome by itself. How we dress those core elements is key to building wagamama dishes and ultimately this kind of cooking is all about uniting a number of different elements to create a whole. Thus honey pork *ramen*, for example, is lent interest by the barbecue sauce used to marinate the pork; in *yasai chilli men* the chilli sauce enhances the delicate flavour of the vegetables; and in *yasai itameru* it is the coconut ginger sauce that gives it oomph.

While these sauces may not form the backbone of the book, they are crucial tools. Increase the amount of ginger used in the coconut ginger sauce, or the amount of spices in the *kare lomen* sauce, and you can greatly influence the spiciness of the finished dish. It is important to remember that these recipes are designed to reflect, in a domestic environment, what we do in the restaurant. Yet as soon as you start to cook these dishes at home they become yours, and your preference may well be for something with a little more or a little less spice. It is the recipes in this chapter that will have the greatest and most immediate impact on the outcome of the finished dishes.

For those of you unfamiliar with Eastern food the presence of sugar may well be a surprise. While in the West we are attuned to the idea that sugar is bad for us, in the East it is more generally seen as another form of seasoning. There is sweetness in many foods and balancing that sweetness with acidity – or sourness – is central to the success of many dishes.

amai sauce

with vinegar, soy and ginger

Essentially a sweet and sour sauce, this is used primarily for dipping. It keeps for a few weeks in the fridge.

makes about 125ml (4fl oz)
1 tablespoon malt vinegar
3 tablespoons sugar
1 tablespoon light soy sauce
1 tablespoon dark soy sauce
pinch of salt
1½ tablespoons tomato ketchup
2 teaspoons tamarind paste

Gently heat the vinegar, sugar and soy sauces in a small pan until the sugar has dissolved. Stir in the remaining ingredients and set aside to cool.

To make tamarind paste: You can buy tamarind paste in ethnic foodstores, either as a concentrate that needs diluting with water, as a paste to use straight up, or in a block. If you buy the block, soak for 1 hour in 500ml (18fl oz) boiling water. Then manipulate the pulp with your fingers to extract as much of it as possible from the seeds and pass through a sieve, discarding what is left in the sieve.

chilli and coriander dressing

You can beef up the chilli to taste, or simply sit back and enjoy the citrus flavour of the coriander spiked with soy and ginger. Use immediately before the coriander wilts.

makes about 125ml (4fl oz)
2 garlic cloves, peeled, chopped and mashed with a little salt
2.5cm (1in) piece of fresh ginger root, peeled and grated
1 red chilli, trimmed and finely chopped
small bunch of coriander, roughly chopped
2 tablespoons fish sauce
3 tablespoons light soy sauce
6 tablespoons vegetable oil

Combine all the ingredients and whisk together.

Much more time is spent chopping and preparing in the kitchens than actually cooking. A whole morning can see vegetables, fish and meat being cut for a lunchtime service, which lasts a couple of hours. In the afternoon the process is repeated all over again.

chilli ramen sauce

with vinegar and nam pla

Spooned over dishes as a finishing sauce, this adds a real meaty kick, to noodles particularly. It will keep for several weeks in the fridge.

makes about 125ml (4fl oz)

2 scant teaspoons sugar
2 tablespoons malt vinegar
3 tablespoons bought sweet chilli sauce
5 tablespoons fish sauce (*nam pla*)

Dissolve the sugar in the vinegar in a small pan over a gentle heat, allow to cool and then combine with the other ingredients.

coconut ginger sauce

with lemongrass and coriander

Stirred into finished dishes this sauce gives a spicy, rich finish and a flavour that is very much of the East. Take care not to over-egg the coconut, it is powerful and can result in the finished dish being too rich. This will keep for about 2 days in the fridge.

makes about 500ml (16fl oz)
4 tablespoons vegetable oil
3 garlic cloves, peeled and finely chopped
2.5cm (1in) piece of fresh ginger root, peeled and grated
2.5cm (1in) piece of galangal, peeled and grated
4 lemongrass sticks, outer leaves removed, finely chopped
500ml (18fl oz) hot water
½ teaspoon salt
2 teaspoons sugar
½ teaspoon *mikku* powder (see page 14)
200g (7fl oz) canned coconut milk
3 tablespoons roughly chopped fresh coriander
salt and white pepper

Heat the oil in a heavy-bottomed frying pan over a low heat. Add the garlic, ginger, galangal and lemongrass. Sauté gently over a moderate heat for 6–8 minutes, stirring until softened and fragrant but not coloured.

Add the hot water, bring to the boil then add the salt, sugar and *mikku* powder. Lower the heat and simmer for a further 20 minutes until reduced by half.

Stir in the coconut milk, heat for a further 2 minutes and remove from the heat. Add the chopped coriander. Check the seasoning before serving and adjust if necessary.

There is nothing to beat fresh coconut. It has a lively, refreshing quality that is never found in a tin or carton. Yet realistically, most of us are not in a position to climb a tree or purchase the real thing every time. Can, carton or block; there is little difference between them.

cucumber dressing

with ginger and chilli

This provides a good kick and a delightful crunch and I find it hard not to eat spoonfuls as I make it. Tossed into crispy leaves it makes for an invigorating, spicy salad.

makes about 500ml (16fl oz)
225ml (8fl oz) rice vinegar
225ml (8fl oz) water
125g (4½oz) sugar
2.5cm (1in) piece of fresh ginger root, peeled and sliced
1 garlic clove, peeled and sliced
salt
225g (8oz) cucumber, grated
6 spring onions, trimmed and thinly sliced
2 chillies, trimmed, deseeded and finely chopped

Put the vinegar, water, sugar, ginger and garlic in a pan and bring to the boil. Season with salt and cook for 2 minutes, stirring until the sugar has dissolved. Leave to cool.

Put the cucumber and spring onions in a bowl and scatter over the chillies. Strain the cooled sauce through a sieve over the cucumber and discard the garlic and ginger. Stir well and store in the fridge for up to 7 days.

Buying the best ingredients, doing as little to them as possible and keeping what cooking time there is to a minimum is all aimed at making everything taste fresh and bright.

chilli sauce

A thick, sweet red sauce spiked with chilli and ginger. This sauce is used to finish dishes off and provides both colour and spice. It will keep for a few days in the fridge.

makes about 300ml (¹/₂ pint)

2 tablespoons vegetable oil

2 lemongrass stalks, outer leaves removed, finely chopped

1 teaspoon peeled and grated fresh ginger root

1 chilli, trimmed and finely chopped

1 red onion, peeled and finely chopped

2 garlic cloves, peeled and finely chopped

½ teaspoon salt

½ teaspoon sugar

1 tablespoon light soy sauce

1 red pepper, trimmed, deseeded and finely chopped

1 tablespoon bought sweet chilli sauce

1 tablespoon tomato ketchup

300ml (½ pint) water

Heat the vegetable oil in a small pan over a low heat until hot. Add the next eight ingredients and sauté for 7–8 minutes without colouring. Add the red pepper and continue cooking gently for 8–10 minutes. Add the remaining ingredients, bring to the boil and simmer for 10 minutes. Blitz in a blender and use.

ebi katsu sauce

with mustard and sesame oil

A fiery finishing or dipping sauce that will keep for up to 10 days in the fridge.

makes about 300ml (¹/₂ pint)

1 tablespoon English mustard powder

1 tablespoon sesame oil

300ml (½ pint) bought sweet chilli sauce

1 tablespoon tomato ketchup

1 tablespoon sugar

Blend the mustard powder and oil until smooth. Add the remaining ingredients and mix thoroughly. Transfer to a small bowl and chill until ready to use.

ebi kuzu kiri sauce

with lime juice

A sharp, intense sauce for finishing or dipping, with lots of citrus flavours balanced by the richness of the oyster sauce. This will keep for up to 10 days in the fridge.

makes about 125ml (4fl oz)
2 teaspoons sugar
2 tablespoons fish sauce (see page 14)
1 tablepoon oyster sauce
juice of 3 limes

Gently heat the sugar and fish sauce until the sugar dissolves. Allow to cool and combine with the oyster sauce and lime juice.

teriyaki sauce

with soy and sake

Primarily used to brush grilled meats, this sauce also adds focus to finished dishes and is great for dipping. It will keep for a few weeks in the fridge. You can also buy various brands of teriyaki sauce.

makes about 125ml (4fl oz)
110g (4oz) sugar
4 tablespoons light soy sauce
2 tablespoons sake
1 teaspoon dark soy sauce

Place the sugar and light soy sauce in a small pan over a low heat and stir until the sugar has dissolved. Simmer for 5 minutes until thick, add the sake and dark soy sauce and allow to cool.

barbecue sauce

By all means pour one out of a bottle, but this coating and finishing sauce really does have much more character and lick-ability. It's the kind of sauce you really don't want to finish.

makes about 200ml (7fl oz)

100ml (3½fl oz) bought yellow bean sauce

100ml (3½fl oz) bought hoi sin sauce

2 teaspoons sugar

2 garlic cloves, peeled and finely minced

1 tablespoon sesame oil

pinch of white pepper

1 tablespoon dark soy sauce

2 tablespoons light soy sauce

Combine all the ingredients together. This will keep in the fridge for several days.

Bench seating means you can spread out or bunch up; couples, groups or singles all get equal billing.

wagamama salad dressing

We have been asked for this recipe more times than any other. Until now we declined to give it out, but the pressure has proved too much!

makes about 125ml (4fl oz)

2 teaspoons finely chopped shallot

2.5cm (1in) piece of fresh ginger root, peeled and grated

1 small garlic clove, peeled and finely chopped

1½ tablespoons rice vinegar

1 tablespoon tomato ketchup

1 tablespoon water

100ml (3½fl oz) vegetable oil

3 tablespoons light soy sauce

Whisk all the ingredients together in a small bowl or screwtop jar and set aside. This can be kept in the fridge for a few days.

Previous page: Making up the wagamama salad dressing. The essence of a good dressing lies in its simplicity; a little too much vinegar or oil and the balance is upset. Confidence is all, along with a little practice.

yaki soba dipping sauce

with soy sauce, sugar and salt

makes about 125ml (4fl oz)

100ml (3½fl oz) light soy sauce

2 teaspoons salt

2 teaspoons sugar

1 teaspoon dark soy sauce

Put all the ingredients in a small pan and bring to the boil. Lower the heat right down and simmer for 10 minutes. Once cool, it will keep for a few weeks in the fridge.

There is a temptation to make dressings and sauces in bulk, but after a few days some tend to lose their freshness and rather than develop their flavour, they start to level out and taste of little. Making up small quantities as and when you need them really is worth it.

soy, sake and ginger marinade

This spicy marinade also doubles as a great dipping sauce for meat, seafood or vegetables. It will keep for up to 5 days in the fridge.

makes about 125ml (4fl oz)

3 tablespoons light soy sauce

3 tablespoons sake or dry sherry

1 tablespoon peeled and grated fresh ginger root

Combine all the ingredients in a small bowl.

gyoza sauce

with garlic, chilli and soy

One of the most useful dipping sauces, all punch and attitude but with a smooth, meaty aftertaste. It will keep for several weeks in the fridge.

makes about 350ml (12fl oz)

1 large garlic clove, peeled and finely chopped

1 large red chilli, trimmed and finely chopped

salt

25g (1oz) sugar

100ml (3½fl oz) malt vinegar

250ml (9fl oz) light soy sauce

1 tablespoon sesame oil

Mash the garlic and chilli together with a little salt with the side of your knife to form a paste. Dissolve the sugar in the vinegar in a small pan over a low heat. Combine everything and store in a sealed container.

Most of the sauces in this chapter are essentially a way of seasoning; of adding something more; another layer. You can dip according to taste, a little or a lot depending on preference. How much you stir into a dish can be varied depending on how you feel. This provides variety, pace and change which means no two examples of a dish are really the same, yet the variation is subtle and controlled.

garlic herb oil

with coriander and parsley

This is a perfect light dressing for fresh, crisp summer salads. The fresher your herbs, the longer your oil will keep.

makes about 250ml (8fl oz)
8 garlic cloves
few sprigs of fresh coriander
few sprigs of fresh flat-leaf parsley
250ml (9fl oz) vegetable oil

Sterilise a suitable glass container by running it through the dishwasher or simmering in boiling water and then drying it on its side in a low oven – about 110°C/225°F/Gas 1/4 for 30 minutes.

Put the garlic, coriander and parsley in the container and add the oil. Cover and store in the fridge to keep the herbs fresh. It will be ready for use in a day and should be used within 10 days.

sweet miso dressing

with sake and mirin

This is a sweet-spicy dressing, which will keep for a few days in the fridge without losing its kick.

makes about 125ml (4fl oz)
2 tablespoons *mirin* (see page 14)
2 tablespoons sake
4 tablespoons sugar
110g (4oz) yellow *miso* paste (see page 14)
1 tablespoon chilli oil (see page 19)
1 tablespoon vegetable oil
2 teaspoons *shichimi* (see page 15)

Put the *mirin* and sake in a small pan and bring to the boil. Lower the heat, add the sugar and stir until dissolved. Pour onto the *miso* paste and beat until smooth. Add the oils and *shichimi* and mix thoroughly.

Both of these dressings have been designed specifically for our dishes, but they work equally well for pretty much any combination of salad ingredients from lettuce to cucumber, radishes to sweet cherry tomatoes.

tsuyu sauce

with soy, mirin and bonito

Tsuyu is a traditional Japanese dipping sauce often eaten with cold *soba* noodles. It can also be bought, but, homemade, it will keep for several weeks in the fridge.

makes about 250ml (8fl oz)
300ml (½ pint) *dashi* (see page 14)
75ml (3fl oz) dark soy sauce
3 tablespoons *mirin* (see page 14)
½ teaspoon sugar
pinch of salt
10g (½ oz) bonito flakes (*katsuo bushi*, see page 14)

Combine all the ingredients except the bonito flakes in a small pan and bring to the boil. Cook over a medium heat for 15 minutes until it has reduced. Remove from the heat, add the bonito flakes and allow to soak for 1 minute. Strain, reserving the bonito for use in soup, if desired, and set aside to cool.

zasai chilli sauce

with shrimp and paprika

Lots of chilli, but you can tone down on the heat if you prefer things a little milder. This delicious finishing sauce will keep for a few days in the fridge.

makes about 250ml (8fl oz)
1 teaspoon dried chilli flakes
1 red onion, chopped
2 garlic cloves, peeled and chopped
200g (7oz) dried shrimp
1 red pepper, trimmed, deseeded and roughly chopped
2 red chillies, trimmed, deseeded and chopped
½ teaspoon paprika
4 tablespoons vegetable oil
3 tablespoons bought sweet chilli sauce
1 teaspoon sugar
½ teaspoon salt

Combine all the ingredients in a blender and blitz to a purée.

yakitori sauce

with soy, sake and mirin

A soy-based dipping and basting sauce, for fish, meat or vegetables.

makes about 200ml (7fl oz)
6 tablespoons sake
180ml (6fl oz) light soy sauce
6 tablespoons *mirin* (see page 14)
1 tablespoon caster sugar

Combine all the ingredients in a small pan and gently heat to dissolve the sugar. Set aside to cool. It will keep indefinitely in the fridge.

When lunch time happens those ramen bowls start shifting off the pass at such a rate even the staff are sometimes surprised. Speed of service is absolutely critical for us and this means in your own kitchen, dishes really do come together in minutes.

yasai vinegar

makes about 250ml (8fl oz)
100g (3½oz) sugar
50ml (2fl oz) water
100ml (3½fl oz) malt vinegar
100ml (3½fl oz) light soy sauce

Dissolve the sugar in the water in a small pan over a low heat. Remove from the heat and add the remaining liquids. Cool, then bottle and seal. The vinegar acts as a souring agent and will keep for a few weeks in the fridge.

kare lomen sauce

with lemongrass and galangal

Inspired by the flavours of Thailand, this sauce works really well with lamb (see page 130). It will keep for a few days in the fridge.

makes about 125ml (4fl oz)

2 lemongrass stalks, outer leaves removed, roughly chopped

2.5cm (1in) piece of galangal, peeled and roughly chopped

2 garlic cloves, peeled and finely chopped

2 onions, peeled and roughly chopped

1 red pepper, trimmed, deseeded and roughly chopped

1 teaspoon sweet paprika

1 teaspoon fennel seeds

½ teaspoon chilli powder

½ teaspoon turmeric

½ teaspoon curry powder

1 teaspoon shrimp paste

Combine all the ingredients in a blender and blitz to a smooth consistency.

Ginger is often given as a possible substitute for galangal, but the two are decidedly different. Galangal has a clean, almost lemony flavour, while ginger is much more soft and rounded. What they do both share however, is an elegant, spicy, peppery taste.

tori kara age sauce

with ginger, soy and sake

Ginger and soy are such a winning combination it is hard not to drizzle this sauce over everything from plain rice and noodles to *gyozas*. It also makes a great marinade for chicken. And the good thing is it will keep indefinitely in the fridge, so you can make lots and have it to hand whenever you need it.

makes about 750ml (1¼ pints)

2.5cm (1in) piece of fresh ginger root, peeled and grated

750ml (1¼ pints) light soy sauce

50ml (2fl oz) sake

1 teaspoon sugar

1 tablespoon oyster sauce

Combine all the ingredients in a pan and heat gently to dissolve the sugar. Set aside to cool.

yasai soba dressing

with lemongrass and ginger

This is a thick dressing, designed to coat noodles rather than salad leaves, although the latter are rather good too. It will keep for months in the fridge.

makes about 250ml (8fl oz)

200g (7oz) teriyaki sauce, homemade (see page 28) or bought

75g (3oz) crushed yellow bean sauce

1 lemongrass stalk, outer leaves removed, finely sliced

1 tablespoon peeled and grated fresh ginger root

Put all the ingredients in a mixing bowl and combine until blended.

3

sides and other small dishes

Eating at wagamama is very informal. Food arrives as it is cooked, making it as fresh and hot as possible. We eschew the traditional structure of starters and mains in favour of a more accessible route. If you fancy a second plate of *gyozas*, it is simple to order and is likely to be delivered in moments. If you are joined by later-comers, they are easily accommodated.

The reasons for this approach are myriad, but chief among them is the more Oriental way of structuring a meal. Several dishes appear on the table at once. The idea is to be as relaxed and easy-going as possible. And the sharing aspect is integral.

As a result of this approach 'sides' is about as far as it goes in terms of first courses. Sides are really things to nibble on while you sip a glass of cold beer, white wine or a juice, or may provide an extra offering for people who are particularly hungry. This chapter is devoted to those dishes that are perfect to serve before you eat, or to accompany a range of other dishes.

We have gained something of a reputation for our *gyozas*: small dumplings filled with combinations of meat, fish and vegetables and presented with various dipping sauces that typically feature a little chilli, ginger perhaps and maybe soy sauce. Most of these sauces will keep for a few days if not weeks in the fridge, so there is no need to make them fresh every time. *Gyozas* can be deep-fried, grilled or steamed. We do them all three ways on the menu for variety, but for cooking at home we'd suggest you find the style you like best and stick with that.

Several recipes feature chicken thigh meat. Minced chicken is not the same thing at all as it tends not to include the brown thigh meat. The best option is to buy thighs and skin and bone them, then chop them into cubes or blitz briefly in a food processor.

Most of the sides featured here are morsels to be picked up using chopsticks or fingers, but there are a few more substantial suggestions. The oven-steamed mussels in sake and ginger (see page 55), for example, is a somewhat larger serving but the idea remains the same: something to eat with the fingers in a relaxed and informal way. A few of the recipes for sides, such as the *gyozas*, are designed for serving more than two people as it is often just not practical to specify the amounts required for such a small number.

The *ebi katsu* (breadcrumbed and shallow-fried prawns, see page 52) are very typical of the bar snacks found around Tokyo, indeed throughout Japan. They are often served alongside *edamame* (soya beans in the pod), which is one of our most popular dishes, the ultimate nibble food and a far cry from peanuts. You may need to go to a specialist store to source them, but very little is required to turn them into an excellent snack (see page 46).

negima yakitori

chargrilled chicken with yakitori sauce

One of our most popular sides. Perfect with an ice-cold beer, the *yakitori* sauce adds a subtle spiciness. A really simple and easy starter.

275g (10oz) boneless, skinless chicken thigh meat (see page 41)
12 spring onions
salt and white pepper
2 tablespoons vegetable oil
4 tablespoons *yakitori* sauce (see page 37)
6 bamboo skewers, soaked in cold water for 2 hours

Cut the chicken into 2.5cm (1in) cubes. Trim the green end and root of the spring onion and cut into 2.5cm (1in) chunks from the root up. Thread the chicken and spring onion pieces alternately onto the skewers (each skewer should have 3 pieces of chicken and 2 pieces of spring onion). Season with salt and white pepper.

Heat a heavy-bottomed frying pan or griddle over a medium heat for 1–2 minutes or until hot and almost smoking and add the oil. Cook the skewers, turning frequently, for about 5–6 minutes until golden brown. Drain on kitchen paper to remove any excess oil and brush with the *yakitori* sauce. Serve immediately.

Talking about the menu and the food: some customers order by number, others less familiar with the menu like to have things explained. There is no formality or structure at wagamama, you order as you like and the food comes as soon as it is ready.

caramelised sweet potatoes

with golden syrup and black sesame seeds

250g (9oz) sweet potato, peeled and cut into thin wedges
vegetable oil, for deep frying
1 teaspoon golden syrup
juice of ½ lemon
1 teaspoon black sesame seeds

Soak the sweet potato wedges for 5 minutes in cold water. Drain well, then pat dry with kitchen paper.

Fill a large pan one-third full of oil and heat to 180°C/350°F or until a cube of bread added to the oil browns in 30 seconds. Carefully lower the wedges into the hot oil and cook for 5 minutes or until golden brown. Remove from the oil and drain well on kitchen paper.

Combine the syrup with the lemon juice and heat in a small saucepan. Pour over the potato wedges, stir well to coat, then transfer to a serving plate and sprinkle with the sesame seeds.

edamame

steamed soya beans with chilli

This recipe is from our restaurants in Sydney where they like things a touch more spicy. In the UK we don't use the oil or the chilli and simply steam the beans for 2 minutes, then add salt. Why not try both versions – either way, the dish is surprisingly morish and makes a great appetiser.

225g (8oz) *edamame*
1 red chilli, trimmed, deseeded and finely chopped
1 teaspoon sesame oil
1 teaspoon salt

Put the *edamame* in a steamer over a pan of salted water and cook for 1–2 minutes, until firm but still with a bite. Drain thoroughly.

   Heat a frying pan until hot and add the chilli and sesame oil. Add the *edamame* and stir fry for 1 minute. Serve, sprinkled with salt, in a bowl and provide another bowl for the shells.

Previous page left: Woked edamame, Australian style. Easy to make, easy to eat: simply hold the pod to your mouth and squeeze. Previous page right: At Wagamama we serve customers; age is not an issue. All are welcome.

miso soup and pickles

with spring onions and wakame

1 tablespoon dried *wakame* (see page 15), soaked in cold water for 5 minutes
500ml (18fl oz) *dashi*, made with *dashi no moto* (see page 14) according to the packet instructions
3 tablespoons *miso* paste (see page 19)
pinch of *mikku* powder (see page 14)
2 spring onions, trimmed and sliced
pickles (see page 15), to serve

Drain the soaked *wakame* and roughly chop. Bring the *dashi* to the boil and whisk in the *miso* paste. Add the *mikku* powder.

   Divide the *wakame* and spring onions between 2 cups or small bowls and pour over the *miso* soup. Serve with a portion (1 scant tablespoonful per person) of mixed pickles.

dashi is a stock based on fish and seaweed. It is key to Japanese cooking and a chef is traditionally judged on its quality. Its simplicity is telling. *Miso* soup is a combination of *dashi* flavoured with *miso*, in our case white *miso* but there are other versions. We also add *wakame* (seaweed) and spring onion. The pickles are traditional and while refrigeration has made the need for pickling largely redundant, in Japan the taste for these crunchy morsels is as strong as ever.

raw salad

mixed leaves with red pepper, cherry tomatoes and wagamama dressing

½ red pepper, trimmed, deseeded and finely sliced

4 handfuls of salad leaves

4 tablespoons wagamama salad dressing (see page 32)

salt and white pepper

6 cherry tomatoes, left whole or halved

6 slices of cucumber

Plunge the pepper slices into iced water until they curl, which will take a few minutes.

Combine the salad leaves with the dressing in a bowl and toss well. Check the seasoning. Divide the leaves between 2 plates and scatter over the tomatoes, cucumber and red pepper.

yasai yakitori

grilled vegetable skewers with yakitori sauce

1 courgette, cut into 2.5cm (1in) slices
3 thick spring onions, bulb end only, cut into 2.5cm (1in) chunks
1 orange pepper, trimmed, deseeded and cut into 2.5cm (1in) chunks
6 button mushrooms
6 cherry tomatoes
2 tablespoons vegetable oil
salt and white pepper
2 tablespoons *yakitori* sauce (see page 37)
6 bamboo skewers, soaked in cold water for 2 hours

Thread 1 piece of vegetable per skewer so each skewer contains 5 pieces. Brush each skewer lightly with vegetable oil and season with salt and white pepper.

Heat a heavy-bottomed frying pan or griddle over a medium heat for 1–2 minutes until hot and almost smoking. Cook the skewers, turning frequently, for 4–5 minutes until golden brown.

Drain on kitchen paper to remove excess oil. Brush with the *yakitori* sauce and serve immediately.

yasai gyoza

steamed vegetable dumplings with soy sauce and sesame oil

Easy to prepare, quick to cook, but you need to make about 30 as it is very hard to get the mixture the correct consistency for less. If you are catering for smaller numbers they will freeze well.

makes about 30

250g (9oz) canned water chestnuts, drained
50g (2oz) white cabbage
10g (½oz) Chinese leaf
1 small carrot
½ onion
1 celery stick
25g (1oz) cornflour
1 tablespoon light soy sauce
1 tablespoon sesame oil
1 teaspoon salt
½ teaspoon sugar
pinch of white pepper
1 packet *gyoza* skins (see page 14)
vegetable oil, for frying
gyoza sauce to serve (see page 33)

Put the water chestnuts, cabbage, Chinese leaf, carrot, onion and celery in a food processor and pulse briefly until finely chopped. (Do not over-process or the mixture will become a pulp.) Using a clean tea towel, gently but firmly squeeze the mixture to remove the excess moisture. Tip into a large bowl and stir in the cornflour, soy sauce, sesame oil, salt, sugar and white pepper.

Put a teaspoonful of the mixture in the centre of each *gyoza* skin. Moisten one of the edges with a little water, then fold over to create a half-moon shape. Press down, to form a neat crescent.

Heat a large frying pan over a medium heat for 1–2 minutes or until hot and almost smoking and add 1 tablespoon of vegetable oil. Put 3 or 4 of the dumplings in the pan and sauté gently for 2 minutes over a low heat until just starting to brown. Don't be tempted to overcrowd the pan or they will stew.

Remove the pan from the heat, add 3 tablespoons of water and cover immediately with a lid or with aluminium foil. Return to the heat for 1 minute, then remove and set aside for a further 2 minutes, by which time the *gyozas* will be heated through. Repeat for the remaining *gyozas*.

Perfect finger food, gyozas are often shared in the restaurants and make great party food. We serve them with a chilli, garlic and soy sauce dip.

ebi gyoza

prawn, soy sauce and sesame dumplings

makes about 30

150g (5oz) cooked peeled prawns

140g (4½oz) canned water chestnuts, drained

2 spring onions, trimmed

110g (4oz) fresh baby spinach leaves

10g (¼oz) cornflour

pinch each of salt, sugar and white pepper

1 teaspoon oyster sauce

1 teaspoon light soy sauce

1 teaspoon sesame oil

1 packet *gyoza* skins (see page 14)

vegetable oil, for frying

gyoza sauce to serve (see page 33)

Gyozas are really easy and fun to make, the secret is not to over-process the filling and to make sure you don't over-fill the skin. Practise makes perfect, as they say.

Put the prawns, water chestnuts and spring onions in a food processor and blitz until finely minced.

Put the spinach in a colander over the sink and wilt by pouring over a kettle of boiling water. Leave to cool and drain, then squeeze gently but firmly to remove the excess water.

Finely chop the spinach and stir into the prawn mixture along with the cornflour, salt, sugar, white pepper, oyster sauce, soy sauce and sesame oil.

Put a teaspoonful of the mixture in the centre of each *gyoza* skin. Moisten one of the edges with a little water then fold over to create a half-moon shape. Press down, to form a neat crescent.

Heat a large frying pan over a medium heat for 1–2 minutes or until hot and almost smoking and add 1 tablespoon of vegetable oil. Put 3 or 4 of the dumplings in the pan and sauté gently for 2 minutes over a low heat until just starting to brown. Don't be tempted to overcrowd the pan or they will stew.

Remove the pan from the heat, add 3 tablespoons of water and cover immediately with a lid or with aluminium foil. Return to the heat for 1 minute, then remove and set aside for a further 2 minutes, by which time the *gyozas* will be heated through. Repeat for the remaining *gyozas*.

ebi katsu

shallow-fried tiger prawns with chilli and garlic dipping sauce

Nobody does breadcrumbs better than the Japanese. They have several grades and the top grade costs serious money. It's all in the texture, crispy but not too heavy. And remember to use a fresh and pure vegetable oil for frying, you want as neutral a flavour as possible.

1 heaped tablespoon flour, seasoned with a pinch of salt
1 egg, beaten
25g (1oz) *panko* breadcrumbs (see page 15)
10 raw tiger prawns, peeled and deveined, tail left on
4 tablespoons vegetable oil
2 tablespoons *ebi katsu* sauce (see page 27)
1 lime, halved, to serve

Put the flour, beaten egg and breadcrumbs into three separate bowls. Dip each prawn first in the flour, then the egg and finally the crumbs. Put on a clean plate lined with kitchen paper and press the crumbs onto the prawns to stop them from falling off. Chill until ready to use.

Heat a heavy-bottomed frying pan over a medium heat for 1–2 minutes or until hot and almost smoking and add the vegetable oil. Shallow fry the prawns in 2 batches, so as not to overcrowd the frying pan, until golden brown on both sides.

Arrange on a plate with a small bowl of the *ebi katsu* sauce and lime halves.

> *Customers often find pronouncing the names of the dishes difficult. We all do. It doesn't matter a bit and that makes me smile.*
> *Una, Dublin*

cured marinated salmon salad

with chilli, lime juice and cucumber

1 teaspoon sugar

juice of 1 lime, plus 2 tablespoons

1 garlic clove, peeled, finely chopped and mashed with a little salt

1 tablespoon sesame oil

3 tablespoons light soy sauce

2 slices (75g/3oz) fresh salmon, cut into 2mm (⅛in) strips

150g (5oz) beansprouts

75g (3oz) cucumber, grated

1–2 red chillies, trimmed and very thinly sliced on the diagonal

2 sprigs of flat-leaf parsley, finely chopped

The 'team' part of the T-shirt logo is central to the wagamama management philosophy of kaizen: everyone concerned with wagamama is actively involved in suggesting and implementing small improvements to the operation.

To make the marinade, combine the sugar and 2 tablespoons of the lime juice in a small bowl and stir until the sugar has dissolved. Add the garlic, sesame oil and soy sauce and stir until emulsified.

Toss the salmon strips in 4 tablespoons of the marinade. Cover and place in the fridge for 3 hours.

To serve, arrange the salmon strips in a flower pattern on 2 plates, working from the outside edge of the plate inwards. Pour the remaining marinade around the plate edge.

Blanch the beansprouts in boiling water for 10 seconds, drain and refresh under cold running water. Shake off the excess water and combine with the cucumber and chilli. Sprinkle with the juice of the whole lime. Pile into the centre of each plate and scatter over the parsley.

oven-steamed mussels

in sake, soy sauce and ginger

500g (1lb 2oz) live mussels
2 leeks, trimmed and julienned
1 red onion, peeled and thinly sliced
1 carrot, peeled and julienned
4 spring onions, trimmed and julienned
1 green chilli, trimmed and thinly sliced
2 garlic cloves, peeled and crushed
1 tablespoon fresh ginger root, peeled and julienned
4 tablespoons sake
2 tablespoons light soy sauce
25g (1oz) butter
2 pieces of turkey foil, 60cm (24in) square

Preheat the oven to 200°C/400°F/Gas 6. Clean and debeard the mussels. Tap any open ones and discard any that do not close. Lay out the squares of foil, shiny side up.

Mix together the mussels and all the vegetables, along with the chilli, garlic and ginger in a large bowl. Divide the mixture into 2, put in the centre of each square and pull up the edges to begin to form a parcel.

Pour over the sake and soy sauce and dot with the butter. Scrunch up the foil edges to form a tightly closed parcel. Put on 2 baking sheets and cook in the oven for 15 minutes or until the mussel shells have opened. Tip into bowls to serve.

Although we don't serve mussels in the restaurants these inexpensive delicacies are perfect for flavouring with the likes of ginger, sake and soy. A more dramatic way of serving them is to present them in the foil, once opened the steam engulfs you with a heady mixture of ginger and soy.

chicken gyoza

chicken, cabbage and chive dumplings with oyster sauce

To say we sell lots of *gyozas* in the restaurants is a bit of an understatement, everyone seems to adore them whether stuffed with prawns, duck, chicken or vegetables.

makes about 30

110g (4oz) Chinese leaf
150g (5oz) white cabbage
100g (3½oz) canned water chestnuts, drained
250g (9oz) boneless, skinless chicken thigh meat, minced (see page 41)
25g (1oz) chives, finely chopped
25g (1oz) cornflour
1 teaspoon sesame oil
1 tablespoon oyster sauce
1 tablespoon light soy sauce
1 teaspoon caster sugar
pinch of salt and white pepper
1 packet *gyoza* skins (see page 14)
vegetable oil, for frying
gyoza sauce to serve (see page 33)

Put the Chinese leaf, cabbage and water chestnuts in a food processor and pulse until finely chopped but not puréed. Using a clean tea towel, squeeze the mixture gently but firmly to remove the excess moisture, then tip into a bowl and add the minced chicken, chives, cornflour, sesame oil, oyster sauce, soy sauce, sugar, salt and white pepper.

Put a teaspoonful of the mixture in the centre of each *gyoza* skin. Moisten one of the edges with a little water, then fold over to create a half-moon shape. Press down, to form a neat crescent.

Heat a large frying pan over a medium heat for 1–2 minutes or until hot and almost smoking and add 1 tablespoon of vegetable oil. Put 3 or 4 of the dumplings in the pan and sauté gently for 2 minutes over a low heat until just starting to brown. Don't be tempted to overcrowd the pan or they will stew.

Remove the pan from the heat, add 3 tablespoons of water and cover immediately with a lid or with aluminium foil. Return to the heat for 1 minute, then remove and set aside for a further 2 minutes, by which time the *gyozas* will be heated through. Repeat for the remaining *gyozas*.

spiced tofu katsu

crispy tofu with sweet chilli sauce

Enticingly spicy with crispy breadcrumbs and soft, creamy tofu underneath; deep-frying is only one of the many ways to cook this versatile ingredient. Tofu, the milk of soya beans, is rich in protein and virtually tasteless, but it works by absorbing all sorts of exciting flavours. It is by no means a modern food and is held in such high regard, some countries refer to it as the 'meat of the fields'.

275g (10oz) firm tofu, cut into 4 equal-sized rectangles, about 1cm (½in) deep
1 tablespoon *shichimi* (see page 15)
1 teaspoon salt
25g (1oz) plain flour
2 eggs, beaten
50g (2oz) *panko* breadcrumbs (see page 15)
vegetable oil, for deep-frying
50ml (2fl oz) bought sweet chilli sauce, for dipping

Pat the tofu cubes dry with kitchen paper to remove the excess water. In a small bowl mix together the *shichimi,* salt and flour. Put the beaten egg in another bowl and the breadcrumbs in a third. Dip the tofu slices first in the spiced flour, then in the beaten egg and finally in the breadcrumbs. Dip them again in the egg and the bread-crumbs for a really good coating.

Fill a large pan one-third full with oil and heat until 180°C/350°F or until a cube of bread added to the oil browns in 30 seconds. Deep fry the coated tofu until golden brown. Drain on kitchen paper. Put onto 2 plates, with a small dish of sweet chilli sauce.

Some consider our restaurants very minimalist in design and while this may be true, it allows the staff to play centre stage, which is a crucial part of how the company is run.

tori kara age

deep-fried chicken with soy, sake and mirin

275g (10oz) boneless, skinless chicken thigh meat, cut into 2.5cm (1in)
   cubes (see page 41)

3 tablespoons *tori kara age* sauce (see page 39)

1 egg, beaten

½ teaspoon dried thyme

½ teaspoon dried oregano

2 teaspoons cornflour

vegetable oil, for deep frying

to serve

2 tablespoons *gyoza* sauce (see page 33)

1 lime, cut into wedges

Marinate the chicken in a shallow bowl in the *tori kara age* sauce for at least 1 hour
and if possible overnight.

In another bowl, mix together the egg, herbs and cornflour until smooth, then add
the marinated chicken pieces and turn to coat thoroughly.

Fill a large pan one-third full with vegetable oil and heat to 180°C/350°F or until
a cube of bread added to the oil browns in 30 seconds. Deep fry the chicken for 5
minutes until golden brown, using a pair of chopsticks or tongs to separate any
cubes that stick together.

Drain on kitchen paper. Serve with a small dish of *gyoza* sauce and a wedge
of lime.

*We have limited the
number of deep-fried
recipes in this book, but
this chicken is too good
to miss out on, crispy
and succulent with a
gentle spicy kick. Finger
food to linger over.*

seared beef sashimi

beef carpaccio and vegetable salad with ginger and coriander

A dish that provides amazing colour as well as taste. In the Sydney restaurants we serve this with *gyoza* sauce (see page 33), which makes a delicious dip.

110g (4oz) fillet steak
salt and white pepper
1 small carrot, peeled and very thinly sliced lengthways
½ cucumber, deseeded and thinly sliced lengthways
4 spring onions, trimmed and thinly sliced
25g (1oz) mangetout, thinly sliced lengthways
½ red onion, peeled and thinly sliced
½ green chilli, trimmed and thinly sliced lengthways
½ red chilli, trimmed and thinly sliced lengthways
½ tablespoon fresh ginger root, peeled and julienned
1½ tablespoons olive oil
1½ tablespoons light soy sauce
4 sprigs of coriander

Season the steak with salt and pepper. Heat a nonstick frying pan until really hot and almost smoking and sear the beef for 15 seconds on each side until golden brown.

Remove from the heat and plunge it into iced water for about 30 seconds. Wrap in clingfilm and place in the freezer for 1 hour to firm up.

Put all the vegetables, chillies and ginger into fresh iced water for 30 minutes to crisp. Remove and drain thoroughly.

To serve, slice the beef into wafer-thin slices and arrange around the edge of a serving plate. Put the vegetable mix in the centre.

Drizzle the olive oil over the steak and vegetables, followed by the soy sauce, and top with the coriander.

4
chicken

I'm walking down a shopping mall in the centre of Tokyo feeling a little hungry. Past the boutiques and electronic shops I'm suddenly hit by the aroma of grilling chicken. The bar is doing a roaring trade in ice-cold beers and the chef is skilfully flipping skewers of chicken on his long chargrill. Time for a break.

Grilled chicken, roast chicken, even poaching chicken is hard to resist, one of those smells that we all associate with comfort and warmth. *Negima yakitori* (see page 42) is one of the most popular sides at wagamama, and chicken features widely on the menu because of its universal popularity.

The Japanese are not traditionally big meat eaters – lack of land is one of the practical reasons for this, but religion and tradition also play their part. Both chicken and duck are popular, not least because the meat cooks quickly. In dishes like chicken chilli *men* and *yaki soba* the speed of cooking means chicken is ideal as a protein element kept in balance with all the other ingredients.

Chicken is widely used in all Asian cooking, its ability to partner ingredients – chilli and other spices, sauces and marinades – making it a fantastic all-rounder. Often it is combined with prawns, an Eastern surf 'n' turf experience that brings a freshness and vitality; our signature dish, wagamama *ramen*, a light, aromatic broth with noodles, chicken, prawns and crabsticks combined with vegetables, is a case in point. A meal in a bowl and very much the way of the noodle.

When buying chicken look out for free-range and, if possible, organic birds. The extra cost should be reflected in the eating; a fuller, more rounded flavour and a firm texture. Chickens are among the most intensively farmed animals and some examples taste of little and come with a decidedly pappy texture. Alternatives include guinea fowl (slightly gamier in flavour and with a firmer flesh) and quail.

The same rules on shopping apply to duck, although the less good examples tend to be very tough and fatty. Seek out a decent supplier and stick to them.

Portion packs offer convenience, but at a price. A whole bird is not difficult to joint and judicious use of the freezer will give you two meals for two people from one bird and a carcass for stock. While breast meat is often heralded as being superior, both leg and thigh meat is often more moist and tends to deliver more flavour (see page 41).

When marinating chicken you need to toss the meat gently in your chosen marinade so it combines. This is best done with your hands or, failing that, use a couple of wooden spoons so the flesh isn't bruised. For the restaurants, chicken is marinated and then sealed in bags to allow the flavours to develop. This technique works well at home too and ensures efficient use of fridge space.

chicken tama rice

chargrilled chicken with oyster sauce and stir fried vegetables

200g (7oz) Japanese or other short-grain rice

2 boneless, skinless chicken breasts

vegetable oil, for frying

salt and white pepper

2 garlic cloves, crushed

1 teaspoon fresh ginger root, grated

1 large courgette, sliced

15 *poku* mushrooms, sliced 5mm (¼in) thick

2 tablespoons *shaoshing* wine (see page 15)

150ml (¼ pint) water

1 teaspoon sugar

2 tablespoons oyster sauce

½ teaspoon cornflour

1 egg, beaten

2 teaspoons sesame oil

Cook the rice in a large pan of boiling water until tender. Set aside.

Preheat the grill or griddle pan. Lightly oil the chicken breasts with vegetable oil, season and grill for 4 minutes on each side, or until cooked through. Allow to rest for 5 minutes, slice on the diagonal and set aside.

Heat a wok over a medium heat for 1–2 minutes or until completely hot and almost smoking and add 3 tablespoons of vegetable oil. Add the garlic and ginger and stir fry for 10 seconds. Add the courgette and mushrooms and stir fry for 1 minute. Pour in the wine and water, then bring to the boil. Add ½ teaspoon salt, the sugar and oyster sauce.

Make a paste with the cornflour and a little cold water, then skim off 2 tablespoons of the liquid in the wok, mix with the paste, return to the pan and bring back to the boil. Add the egg to the sauce and cook until soft but don't let it curdle. Stir through the sesame oil.

Divide the rice between 2 plates, place the chargrilled chicken breast on top, and pour on the sauce.

chicken chilli men

stir fried chicken with green pepper, spring onions and noodles

275g (10oz) *soba* noodles
3 tablespoons vegetable oil
2 boneless, skinless chicken breasts, cut on the diagonal into 1cm (½in) strips
1 green pepper, trimmed, deseeded and thinly sliced
1 small courgette, thinly sliced
½ red onion, peeled and thinly sliced
4 spring onions, trimmed and cut into 2.5cm (1in) lengths
300ml (½ pint) chilli sauce (see page 27)

Cook the noodles in a large pan of boiling water for 2–3 minutes or until just tender. Drain thoroughly and refresh under cold water.

Heat a wok over a medium heat for 1–2 minutes or until completely hot and almost smoking and add the vegetable oil. Add the chicken, pepper, courgette, red onion and spring onion and stir fry for 3–4 minutes until the chicken is cooked and the vegetables are lightly coloured. Add the chilli sauce and bring to the boil. Divide the noodles between 2 bowls and top with the stir fry.

cha han

stir fried chicken and prawns with sweetcorn, mushrooms and fragrant rice

200g (7oz) boneless, skinless chicken thigh meat (see page 41)
2 tablespoons *yakitori* sauce (see page 37)
2 tablespoons vegetable oil
8 cooked, peeled prawns
2 tablespoons canned sweetcorn, well drained
2 tablespoons mangetout, finely sliced
4 button mushrooms, finely sliced
2 spring onions, trimmed and cut into 2.5cm (1in) lengths
2 eggs, beaten
75g (3oz) cooked Thai fragrant rice
salt
2 tablespoons light soy sauce
miso soup and pickles (see page 46), to serve

Combine the chicken and the *yakitori* sauce in a bowl. Work gently with your fingers for a few minutes, turning the meat in the sauce. Marinate for at least 30 minutes (1 hour is even better). Remove the chicken, reserving the marinade, and cut the meat on the diagonal into thin slices.

Heat a wok over a medium heat for 1–2 minutes or until completely hot and almost smoking and add the vegetable oil. Add the prawns, sweetcorn, mangetout, mushrooms and spring onions along with the chicken and stir fry over a medium heat for about 5 minutes until the vegetables just start to wilt and the chicken is cooked. Add the egg and continue to stir fry until it is just scrambled.

Add the rice. Season with salt and soy sauce and continue stir frying until everything is mixed evenly and the rice heated through. Divide between 2 bowls and serve with *miso* soup and pickles.

cha han is easily one of the most popular dishes on the menu. With lots of vegetables, its light seasoning of *yakitori* sauce and ever-popular chicken and prawns the combination seems to be a winner with young and old alike – my son says it's definitely his favourite. All the preparation for this dish happens up-front. Cooking is really a matter of minutes and the whole assembly can be on the table in less than 20.

chicken ramen

chargrilled chicken and noodle soup with pak choi and bamboo

Combine noodles, hot stock, fresh vegetables and lightly grilled chicken and you have a complete meal in a bowl. Fast food really doesn't get better than this.

2 boneless, skinless chicken breasts
vegetable oil, for oiling
salt and white pepper
250g (9oz) *ramen* noodles
1 litre (1¾ pints) chicken or vegetable stock (see pages 17 and 18)
2 pak choi, trimmed and roughly chopped (or 2 handfuls of baby
   spinach leaves)
12 pieces *menma* (canned bamboo shoots), drained
4 spring onions, trimmed and finely sliced

Preheat the grill or griddle pan. Lightly oil and season the chicken breasts and grill for 4 minutes on each side, or until cooked through. Allow to rest for 5 minutes, slice on the diagonal and set aside.

Cook the noodles in a large pan of boiling water for 2–3 minutes until just tender. Drain, refresh under cold running water and divide between 2 bowls.

Heat the chicken or vegetable stock until boiling. Put the pak choi on top of the noodles and ladle in the stock. Top with the sliced chicken, *menma* and spring onions.

Thank you. I am a devoted fan. Could you please send me the recipe for chicken ramen. I could eat it forever!
Trey, USA

ginger chicken teppan

stir fried chicken and noodles with chilli, coriander and ginger

200g (7oz) *udon* noodles

handful of mangetout, finely sliced

½ red onion, peeled and thickly sliced

4 spring onions, trimmed and cut into 2.5cm (1in) lengths

1 garlic clove, peeled and finely sliced

1 tablespoon fresh ginger root, peeled and grated

2 tablespoons roughly chopped coriander

1 red chilli, deseeded and finely sliced

2 handfuls of beansprouts

3 tablespoons *tsuyu* sauce (see page 36)

2 eggs, beaten

2 tablespoons vegetable oil

300g (10½oz) boneless, skinless chicken thigh meat, cut into strips

2 teaspoons pickled ginger *(gari*, see page 14*)*

6 sprigs of coriander

Cook the noodles in a large pan of boiling water for 2–3 minutes or until just tender. Drain and refresh under cold running water. Put all the ingredients except the oil, chicken, pickled ginger and coriander sprigs in a large bowl, adding in the noodles last, and mix to combine.

Heat a wok over a medium heat for 1–2 minutes or until completely hot and almost smoking and add the vegetable oil. Add the chicken and stir fry for 5 minutes, or until cooked. Add everything from the bowl and stir fry for 3–4 minutes. Check the seasoning, then divide the stir fry between 2 plates and scatter over the pickled ginger and coriander sprigs.

Beansprouts may not major on the flavour front, but their crunchy texture is a key aspect in many stir fry dishes and salads.

pre-cooking or buying pre-cooked noodles means you have much more control when it comes to completing the dish. It is a small but necessary step. When it comes to 'the way of the noodle' the idea is to make slurping noises whilst eating – the extra oxygen enhances the flavour of the dish. The truth is it is very difficult to eat noodles with chopsticks and do other-wise. Napkins are to be advised and reducing the distance from bowl to mouth also helps. In Japan the bowl is often held up close to the face and is the reason why the bowls are not made from china – they would simply get too hot.

chicken and prawn hot pot

with tofu, mushrooms and soy sauce

This recipe is a real reviver – soothing, comforting and gentle. A reminder how very subtle and delicate Japanese food can be.

600ml (1 pint) *dashi*, made with *dashi no moto* (see page 14) according to
   packet instructions
2 tablespoons sake
1 tablespoon light soy sauce
pinch of salt
2 teaspoons *mirin* (see page 14)
225g (8oz) boneless, skinless chicken thigh meat, cut into 2.5cm (1in) cubes
4 shiitake mushrooms, roughly chopped
2 Chinese leaves, cut into 2.5cm (1in) wide strips
4 spring onions, trimmed and cut into 2cm (¾in) lengths
5 x 2.5cm (1in) cubes firm tofu
250g (9oz) white *ramen* noodles
small bunch of Chinese chives
4 cooked tiger prawns, unpeeled

Put the *dashi*, sake, soy sauce, salt and *mirin* in a pan and bring to the boil. Add the chicken, cover and lower the heat. Simmer for 3 minutes until the chicken is almost cooked through. Add the remaining ingredients, except for the prawns, and cook for a further 2–3 minutes. Remove from the heat, add the prawns and set aside for 2 minutes to heat the prawns through. Divide between 2 bowls.

Central to wagamama is the idea of a long kitchen and bench seating which is perpendicular to it. It means food can be delivered at speed without any fuss. This broke away from the traditional concept of a restaurant kitchen and dining room being separate elements – the constant noise and buzz of the kitchen is all part of the wagamama experience.

teriyaki chicken stir fry

with chilli, garlic, spring onion and rice

250g (9oz) boneless, skinless chicken breast or thigh meat (see page 41),
   sliced into 1cm (½in) strips
1 red chilli, trimmed and finely sliced
1 teaspoon garlic paste (homemade or bought)
4 tablespoons teriyaki sauce, homemade (see page 28) or bought
2 tablespoons vegetable oil
110g (4oz) beansprouts
½ red onion, peeled and thickly sliced
½ red pepper, trimmed, deseeded and cut into strips
75g (3oz) pak choi, halved
pinch of salt
pinch of sugar
1 spring onion, trimmed and finely sliced on the diagonal
cooked plain boiled rice, to serve

Place the chicken, chilli, garlic paste and teriyaki sauce in a large bowl or clean plastic bag and mix thoroughly. Cover and marinate in the fridge for 2–3 hours.

Heat a wok over a medium heat for 1–2 minutes or until completely hot and almost smoking and add the oil. Add the chicken and any marinade from the bowl, and stir fry for about 5 minutes until all the meat is golden. Continue cooking for a further minute, then add the beansprouts, red onion, red pepper and pak choi.

Stir fry for a further 2 minutes, ensuring the base of the wok doesn't burn (you can add a teaspoon of water during this time to take some of the heat out of the wok). Season to taste with salt and sugar. Divide between 2 plates, top with spring onion slices and serve with the rice.

positive eating and living drives the menu and defines what wagamama is all about. Wagamama means wilfulness or self-ishness: selfishness in terms of looking after oneself, looking after oneself in terms of positive eating and positive living. Before wagamama, fast food implied a compromise. The idea of providing well-cooked, well-presented nutritious meals prepared to order in comfortable surroundings had never been achieved on this scale before.

yaki udon

stir fried chicken with shiitake mushrooms, leek and red pepper

200g (7oz) boneless, skinless chicken thigh meat (see page 41)

2 tablespoons *yakitori* sauce (see page 37)

200g (7oz) *udon* noodles

1 egg

2 tablespoons *yaki soba* sauce (see page 32)

2 tablespoons curry oil (see page 19)

4 shiitake mushrooms, sliced

75g (3oz) leeks, finely chopped

150g (5oz) beansprouts

1 red pepper, trimmed, deseeded and cut into thin batons

6 x 5mm (¼in) pieces mini *chikuwa* (see page 14)

4 cooked and peeled prawns

2 tablespoons vegetable oil

2 tablespoons dried shallots

1 tablespoon spicy fish powder (see page 15)

1 teaspoon pickled ginger (*gari*, see page 14)

Combine the chicken and the *yakitori* sauce in a bowl. Work gently with your fingers for a few minutes, turning the meat in the sauce. Set aside for at least 30 minutes (1 hour is even better). Remove, reserving the sauce, and cut the chicken into thin slices.

Cook the noodles in a large pan of boiling water for 2–3 minutes or until just tender. Drain and refresh under cold running water. Crack the egg into a large bowl and beat in the *yaki soba* sauce and curry oil. Toss in all the vegetables, *chikuwa*, prawns and noodles and mix until thoroughly combined.

Heat a wok over a medium heat for 1–2 minutes or until completely hot and almost smoking and add the oil. Add the chicken and any remaining sauce and stir fry for 3–4 minutes or until cooked. Add the egg and vegetable mixture and stir fry for 4–5 minutes until everything is just tender. Divide between 2 plates and top with the shallots, fish powder and pickled ginger.

Marinating chicken gives the meat much more flavour and the dish over-all, a much 'bigger' taste. By far the best way to do this is to make up the marinade and place it in a plastic bag with the meat. Massage gently with your hands and set aside in a cool place, overnight if possible.

wagamama ramen

seasonal greens with prawns, crabstick, tofu and chicken

If we have a signature dish this is probably the one. Universally popular it epitomises what wagamama is all about. Simple ingredients simply prepared yet delivering oodles of flavour in a nutritious way. This is one of the all-time favourites, a take on the classic noodle dishes eaten at stalls throughout Japan and the inspiration for the first wagamama restaurant.

150g (5oz) firm tofu
vegetable oil, for frying
250g (9oz) *ramen* noodles
4 slices *kamaboko-aka* (see page 14)
4 crabsticks
1 egg, hard-boiled
4 cooked and peeled prawns
2 pak choi, roughly chopped
1 litre (1¾ pints) chicken stock (see page 17)
2 boneless, skinless chicken breasts
salt and white pepper
12 pieces *menma* (canned bamboo shoots), drained
1 tablespoon *wakame* (see page 15), soaked in warm water for 5 minutes,
    drained and roughy chopped
2 spring onions, trimmed and finely sliced

Cut the tofu into 1cm (½in) slices and pan fry in a little oil for about 1 minute on each side until just coloured.

Cook the noodles in a large pan of boiling water for 2–3 minutes or until just tender, drain, refresh under cold running water and drain again. Divide between 2 bowls along with the *kamaboko-aka*, crabsticks, tofu, half an egg each, 2 prawns each and the pak choi.

Bring the chicken stock to the boil. Preheat the grill or a griddle. Lightly coat the chicken breasts in vegetable oil, season with salt and pepper and grill or chargrill for 4 minutes each side or until cooked. Allow to rest for 5 minutes and slice on the diagonal into 1cm (½in) strips.

To serve, pour the chicken stock over the noodles, lay the chicken strips on top and garnish with the *menma, wakame* and spring onion slices.

miso ramen

miso soup with chicken, leek, bamboo shoots and ramen noodles

Miso is a magical food. Made from soya beans and grain, it is similar to yoghurt in having living enzymes and has an almost mystical status in Japanese cuisine. There are several different types but personal preference should be the deciding factor. Experiment until you find one you like.

250g (9oz) *ramen* noodles
1 litre (1¾ pints) chicken stock (see page 17)
110g (4oz) *miso* paste (see page 19)
150g (5oz) boneless, skinless chicken, cut on the diagonal
   into strips 1cm (½in) wide
1 egg, beaten
1 tablespoon cornflour
salt and white pepper
2 tablespoons vegetable oil
2 garlic cloves, peeled and crushed
1 small carrot, peeled and shredded
½ leek, finely sliced
large handful of beansprouts
2 teaspoons sugar
2 tablespoons light soy sauce
12 pieces *menma* (canned bamboo shoots), drained
handful of *wakame* (see page 15), soaked in warm water
   for 5 minutes, drained and roughly chopped
1 teaspoon chilli oil (see page 19)
1 teaspoon sesame seeds, toasted (see page 164)

Cook the noodles in a large pan of boiling water for 2–3 minutes or until just tender. Drain and refresh under cold running water. Place the stock in a pan and bring to the boil. Whisk in the *miso* paste until free of lumps. Cover and remove from the heat.

Combine the chicken, egg, cornflour and a seasoning of salt and pepper.

Heat a wok over a medium heat for 1–2 minutes or until completely hot and almost smoking and add the vegetable oil. Add the garlic, stir fry for 5 seconds, then add the chicken, carrot, leek and beansprouts and stir fry for 3–4 minutes or until slightly caramelised. Add 1 teaspoon salt, the sugar and soy sauce and cook for 1 minute.

Divide the noodles between 2 bowls and ladle over the stock. Top with the vegetables, *menma, wakame*, chilli oil and sesame seeds.

Preparation is key to cooking the food in this book. Lots of chopping and organising before the cooking actually takes place. This can mean ingredients lists look long, but a lot will come out of your cupboard and what you do need to buy is generally easy to carry home. A good chopping board and sharp knife are essential, but these few utensils mean there is very little washing up.

chicken rice noodles

with chilli and coconut ginger sauce

100g (3½oz) rice noodles
350ml (12fl oz) coconut ginger sauce
  (see page 25)
3 tablespoons vegetable oil
200g (7oz) boneless, skinless chicken breast, cut on the
  diagonal into strips 1cm (½in) wide
2 red chillies, trimmed and finely sliced
1 small onion, peeled and roughly chopped
handful of beansprouts
½ red pepper, trimmed, deseeded and finely sliced
½ teaspoon salt
½ teaspoon sugar
2 tablespoons light soy sauce
few sprigs of coriander
1 lime, halved, to serve

Cook the noodles in a large pan of boiling water for 2–3 minutes until just tender. Drain and return to the saucepan. Stir in the coconut ginger sauce. Toss well to coat the noodles in the sauce. Cover with a tea towel and set aside.

Heat a wok over a medium heat for 1–2 minutes or until completely hot and almost smoking and add the vegetable oil. Add the chicken and stir fry for 2–3 minutes or until just cooked through. Add the chillies, onion, beansprouts and red pepper and continue to stir fry for a further 3 minutes or until the vegetables are beginning to soften. Season with salt, sugar and soy sauce and continue to stir fry for a further minute.

Divide the noodles between 2 bowls and top with the stir fry and the coriander. Serve with a wedge of lime.

Using a wok is relatively easy, but practice is a good idea. Make sure it is well heated – best done over a medium flame for 1 or 2 minutes – then turn the heat up and add the oil, quickly followed by the first group of ingredients.

stir fries are an incredibly quick way to cook and the short time means all the ingredients retain most of their texture, flavour and nutrients. The idea is to constantly toss the contents so they stir fry rather than fry, which is why a large flame is needed to keep the heat as the ingredients move around the wok. You can substitute other poultry for the chicken or vary the vegetables depending on what you have to hand. We are specific in the restaurants about what goes into a dish, but at home there is lots of leeway to experiment and extend the basic recipe.

marinated chicken stir fry

with peanuts, lemongrass, soy sauce and coriander

2 boneless, skinless chicken breasts, cut on the diagonal into
strips 1cm (½in) wide
2 lemongrass stalks, tough outer leaves removed, very thinly sliced
2–3 red chillies, trimmed and sliced
2 garlic cloves, peeled and crushed
3 tablespoons vegetable oil
2 tablespoons fish sauce (see page 14)
1 small red onion, peeled and cut into 1cm (½in) strips
12 mangetout
2 handfuls of beansprouts
½ green pepper, trimmed, deseeded and cubed
1 teaspoon salt
1 teaspoon sugar
4 tablespoons salted peanuts, chopped
3 tablespoons light soy sauce
300ml (½ pint) water
2 tablespoons cornflour
300g (10½oz) steamed rice
few sprigs of coriander, chopped

Put the chicken strips, lemongrass, chilli, garlic, 1 tablespoon of the vegetable oil and the fish sauce in a large bowl. Mix thoroughly, cover and refrigerate overnight.

Heat a wok over a medium heat for 1–2 minutes or until completely hot and almost smoking and add the remaining oil and the red onion. Stir fry for 1 minute until lightly caramelised. Add the chicken and its marinade and continue stir frying for 1 minute to seal the meat. Add the mangetout, beansprouts and green pepper. Continue stir frying for a further 2 minutes or until the vegetables start to wilt. Add the salt, sugar and half the peanuts and stir fry for a further minute.

Add the soy sauce and water. Mix the cornflour with 2 tablespoons water to make a paste. Remove 2 tablespoons of the sauce from the wok, combine with the corn-flour paste, return to the wok and toss well. Continue cooking for a further 4–5 minutes until the sauce is thick and glossy.

Press the cooked rice into a cup and invert onto 2 plates. Spoon over the stir fry, scatter with the remaining peanuts and chopped coriander.

zasai chicken gohan

stir fried chicken with Szechuan vegetables, oyster sauce, and sesame oil

1½ tablespoons vegetable oil

200g (7oz) boneless, skinless chicken breast, cut into strips

1 garlic clove, peeled and crushed

25g (1oz) pickled cabbage, soaked in cold water for
    15 minutes, then drained

25g (1oz) Szechuan vegetables (see page 15), soaked in cold water for
    15 minutes, then drained

4 shiitake mushrooms, sliced

4 spring onions, trimmed and cut into 2.5cm (1in) lengths

150ml (¼ pint) water

2 teaspoons sugar

1 tablespoon oyster sauce

1 teaspoon salt

2 teaspoons light soy sauce

½ teaspoon cornflour

pinch of white pepper

1 egg, beaten

2 teaspoons sesame oil

350g (12oz) cooked Japanese short-grain rice

2 teaspoons *zasai* chilli sauce (see page 36)

Heat a wok over a medium heat for 1–2 minutes or until completely hot and almost smoking and add the vegetable oil. Add the chicken and stir fry for 3 minutes or until it loses its colour. Add the garlic and stir fry for 5 seconds, then add the pickled vegetables, mushrooms and spring onions. Stir fry for a further 5 seconds and add the water, sugar, oyster sauce, salt and soy sauce.

Bring to the boil and remove any froth with kitchen paper. Mix together the cornflour with 1 tablespoon cold water, the white pepper and egg and, when smooth, add to the sauce to thicken. Bring almost to the boil and stir through the sesame oil.

Divide the rice between 2 plates and add the stir fried chicken. Top with the *zasai* chilli sauce.

5
fish

Tsukiji market, the central fish market in Tokyo, is the largest fish market in the world. I've never seen so much tuna: rows and rows of both fresh and frozen with numbers slapped on to the sides. Quality is everything to the Japanese and some of these tuna are fetching serious prices; arm-waving, constant shouting and lots of facial expressions do the communicating. I'm simply mesmerised by the fish.

The market is huge and when I tear myself away from the tuna there is everything else you can think of to view: sea bass and sea bream, salmon and squid and every size of prawn imaginable.

Fish is a key source of protein in the Japanese diet; for a small country surrounded by the sea it was an obvious choice over land-demanding animals like cattle and sheep. At wagamama we serve a total of over 1,000kg (2,200lb) of prawns, salmon and crabsticks every week, a figure which keeps increasing.

Top of the list for our customers is the seafood *ramen*, a rich and satisfying broth with noodles and prawns, crabsticks and squid. It comes with *menma* (pickled bamboo shoots) and *kamaboko-aka*, a small fishcake. The addition of a pickle with fish is very traditional in Japanese cuisine. Alternatives include *gari* (pickled ginger) and *daikon* (white radish).

Many of the wagamama specials are fish based and the following chapter reflects this emphasis. Cod baked in foil, teriyaki sea bass, monkfish *yakitori* – all of these have at one time or another featured on the wagamama menu. But we have also included a few extras: the mackerel with soy and ginger (see page 115), for example, is a great way to serve this much underrated and very healthy fish and the salmon hot pot (see page 108) is another homely, comforting dish not suited to the busy service needs of the restaurants but one which sits very firmly in the more robust style of Japanese home cooking.

notes on buying fish Freshness is all when buying fish. Don't be afraid to prod and poke, to question and examine. Ask leading questions: 'Is this fresh?' will invariably get a yes, whereas 'How fresh is this?' requires a little more thought on the part of your fishmonger. An increasing amount of fish we buy is now farmed; unless it states otherwise this is largely true of most of the salmon, sea bass and sea bream on sale. Farmed fish can be excellent, but its quality can vary hugely and some of it is decidedly below par.

ebi yakitori

stir fried vegetable skewers with grilled prawns and dipping sauce

18 raw peeled prawns

1 courgette, cut into 2.5cm (1in) slices

1 orange pepper, trimmed, deseeded and cut into 2.5cm (1in) chunks

6 thick spring onions, trimmed and cut into 2.5cm (1in) chunks

6 button mushrooms

6 cherry tomatoes

4 tablespoons *ebi kuzu kiri* sauce (see page 28)

110g (4oz) *soba* noodles

4 spring onions, trimmed and finely sliced

large handful of beansprouts

2 garlic cloves, peeled and crushed with a little salt

1 teaspoon salt

1 heaped teaspoon sugar

2 tablespoons vegetable oil

6 wooden skewers, soaked in cold water for 2 hours

Thread 3 prawns on each skewer, alternating with 1 piece of courgette, 2 pieces of pepper, 2 pieces of thick spring onion, 1 mushroom and 1 tomato. Brush with some of the *ebi kuzu kiri* sauce. Preheat the grill or a griddle and cook the *yakitori* for 3–4 minutes, turning frequently, until the prawns are cooked through.

Cook the noodles in a large pan of boiling water for 2–3 minutes until just tender. Drain thoroughly, then combine in a large bowl with the finely sliced spring onions, beansprouts, garlic, salt and sugar. Heat a large, heavy-bottomed frying pan or wok and add the vegetable oil. Add the noodle mixture and stir fry for 2 minutes until all the ingredients are combined and warmed through. Transfer to 2 plates and top with the cooked prawn *yakitori*. Drizzle over the remaining sauce.

It takes quite a while for a griddle pan to reach optimal heat. Too hot and everything will simply burn, not hot enough and what you lay on top will stew and fail to pick up those attractive lines. Keep the heat moderate to hot, and allow a good few minutes for it to reach temperature.

amai udon

stir fried noodles with prawns, tofu and leek

400g (14oz) *udon* noodles
2 eggs, beaten
75ml (3fl oz) *amai* sauce (see page 22)
1 large leek, trimmed and finely sliced
6 cooked peeled prawns
large handful of beansprouts
2 tablespoons vegetable oil
110g (4oz) firm tofu, cut into 10 cubes
juice of 1 lime
2 tablespoons chopped roasted peanuts

Cook the noodles in a large pan of boiling water for 2–3 minutes until just tender. Drain, refresh under cold running water and reserve.

Put the egg and the *amai* sauce in a large bowl and stir in the leek, prawns, beansprouts and noodles. Heat a wok over a medium heat for 1–2 minutes or until completely hot and almost smoking and add the vegetable oil. Add the tofu and stir fry for 2 minutes or until starting to colour.

Tip the contents of the bowl into the wok and stir fry for 3–4 minutes until the egg is cooked and the leeks are softened.

Divide between 2 bowls, squeeze over some lime juice and scatter with the chopped peanuts.

stir fries are one of the most popular cooking methods in our house. My children enjoy the speed as well as the contents. What I really relish is everything tasting its best. Minimal cooking means the mangetout still have crunch as well as flavour, the carrots are still sweet as well as crunchy and the prawns have a succulence and sea-salty tang which delights. The lack of washing up also encourages me, but that is to dwell on the mundane.

ebi chilli men

stir fried prawns with green pepper, carrots and soba noodles

1 egg
1 teaspoon sesame oil
pinch of white pepper
1 tablespoon cornflour
12 raw peeled prawns
2 tablespoons vegetable oil
1 green pepper, trimmed, deseeded and cut into chunks
2 carrots, peeled and sliced on the diagonal
300ml (½ pint) chilli sauce (see page 27)
250g (9oz) *soba* noodles

Combine the egg, sesame oil, white pepper and cornflour in a bowl, whisk to form a smooth mixture and gently stir in the prawns.

Heat a wok over a medium heat for 1–2 minutes or until completely hot and almost smoking and add the vegetable oil. Add the green pepper and carrot and stir fry for 2–3 minutes or until just tender. Add the prawns, stir fry for 30 seconds, then add the chilli sauce and bring to the boil. Simmer for 2 minutes, remove from the heat and set aside while you cook the noodles.

Cook the noodles in a large pan of boiling water for 2–3 minutes until just tender. Drain and divide between 2 plates. Top with the prawns and sauce.

Shell-on prawns tend to deliver more flavour and texture than their iced-up shell-off cousins. Preparation is slightly more fiddly, but is not that onerous and you can always get somebody to work on this alongside you. If you sauté the shells in the vegetable oil and then discard the shells before you start cooking it will enhance the flavour of the finished dish.

grilled sea bream

with soy sauce and stir fried garlic noodles

The tang of soy sauce partnered with the nutty, almost sweet flavour of sesame oil is more than a match for this meatiest of fish.

2 x 150g (5oz) sea bream fillets, scaled
2 tablespoons light soy sauce
1 teaspoon sesame oil
110g (4oz) *soba* noodles
4 spring onions, cut into 2.5cm (1in) lengths
2 teaspoons garlic paste (homemade or bought)
handful of beansprouts
1 teaspoon salt
1 teaspoon sugar
2 tablespoons vegetable oil

Put the sea bream in a shallow dish and cover with the soy sauce and sesame oil. Cover, then put in the fridge for 2 hours.

Preheat the grill to medium-high. Cook the noodles in a large pan of boiling water for 2–3 minutes until just tender. Drain thoroughly and refresh under cold water, then combine with the spring onions, garlic, beansprouts, salt and sugar in a large bowl.

Put the sea bream on a baking sheet skin-side up, reserving the excess marinade. Grill for 5 minutes until cooked through.

Heat a wok over a medium heat for 1–2 minutes or until completely hot and almost smoking and add the vegetable oil. Add the noodles and stir fry for 2 minutes until all the ingredients are heated through, adding in the reserved marinade. Divide the noodles between 2 plates and top with the sea bream.

grilled teriyaki sea bass

with mixed leaves and garlic rice

2 x 150g (5oz) sea bass fillets, scaled
4 tablespoons teriyaki sauce, homemade (see page 28) or bought
175g (6oz) rice
1 tablespoon vegetable oil
pinch of salt
large handful of mixed salad leaves
1 tablespoon shredded carrot or *daikon* (mooli)
4 tablespoons garlic herb oil (see page 35)

Place the sea bass fillets in a bowl with 2 tablespoons of the teriyaki sauce. Toss gently and set aside. Cook the rice in a pan of boiling water for 8 minutes (or according to the packet instructions) until just tender, then drain.

Heat a griddle until really hot and lightly oil with kitchen paper dipped in vegetable oil. Season the sea bass with the salt, then cook, skin-side down, for 2 minutes. Turn over and cook for 1 minute until done.

Press the rice into a cup and invert onto 2 plates. Combine the salad leaves and carrot or *daikon* and place a handful alongside the rice. Drizzle over the garlic herb oil along with 1 tablespoon of the teriyaki sauce for each plate. Top with the sea bass and a little extra teriyaki sauce.

For the love of God, open a wagamama in New York!
Mike, USA

home-cured spiced swordfish steak

grilled swordfish, ramen noodles and baby vegetables

Vegetables poached in a light stock, the gutsy flavour of just-cooked swordfish and the soothing comfort of noodles. Simplicity at its best and everything tasting of itself; pure and easy.

2 scant teaspoons coarse sea salt

2 x 175g (6oz) swordfish steaks

pinch of ground black pepper

1 teaspoon finely chopped garlic

1 red chilli, trimmed and sliced

2 sprigs of coriander, finely chopped

1 tablespoon lime juice

1 litre (1¾ pints) vegetable stock (see page 18)

75g (3oz) baby vegetables (sweetcorn, sugarsnap peas
   or mangetout)

300g (10½oz) *ramen* noodles

a little vegetable oil

4 spring onions, trimmed and sliced

Line a tray with clingfilm, place half the salt on the clingfilm and put the swordfish on top. Cover with the remaining salt, the black pepper, garlic, sliced red chilli and coriander. Pour over the lime juice. Cover with more clingfilm and place another tray with weights (or something heavy) on it and leave to marinate overnight in the fridge.

The following day, heat the stock and cook the baby vegetables for 2–3 minutes or until tender. Cook the noodles in a large pan of boiling water for 2–3 minutes until just tender, then drain thoroughly. Divide between 2 bowls and ladle over the stock and vegetables.

Brush the salt mixture off the swordfish. Heat a griddle, lightly oil using kitchen paper dipped in vegetable oil and cook the swordfish for 2–3 minutes on each side or until opaque right through. Slice the steaks, place on top of the noodles and sprinkle over the spring onion slices.

Oil the griddle pan lightly to avoid a kitchen full of smoke. Some fumes are inevitable, but the idea is to be able to see what you are doing and not be arguing with the fire brigade.

fish is surely the ultimate fast food for those of us interested in real food; easy to prepare, quick to cook and full of texture and flavour. No wonder this is the largest chapter in the book. Fish is an ingredient as friendly to a wok as a saucepan of hot broth, up for marinating as keenly as being seared in a pan of hot oil.

poached cod with shiitake

and soy sauce

25g (1oz) butter

2 x 150g (5oz) cod fillets

2 spring onions, trimmed and finely sliced

¼ green pepper, trimmed, deseeded and cut into thin strips

handful of shiitake mushrooms, finely sliced

1 tablespoon sake

salt and white pepper

2 teaspoons light soy sauce

2 x aluminium foil squares approximately three times the size of the cod fillets

to serve

mixed salad leaves

steamed rice or glass vermicelli

Preheat the oven to 200°C/400°F/Gas 6. Lay the foil squares on a board, shiny-side down. Using half the butter, grease an area just larger than the size of the cod fillets.

Put the cod on the foil, skin-side down, and top with the spring onions, green pepper and shiitake mushrooms. Dot with the remaining butter and the sake and season with salt and pepper.

Wrap the foil tightly to form a sealed parcel. Put in a roasting tray and pour in enough hot water to come half way up the sides. Place in the centre of the oven for about 10 minutes, or until cooked. Open the parcels carefully and drizzle in the soy sauce. Serve with a simple salad and steamed rice or glass vermicelli.

Butter, soy and sake are a winning combination. They shouldn't work – butter is hardly an Eastern ingredient – but prize open the sealed tin foil after cooking and you will be enveloped in a cloud of steam heady with rich and exotic aromas.

sweet miso cod

grilled marinated cod, black sesame seeds and seaweed rice

Miso lends this dish an unmistakably meaty quality making it somehow much bigger. Which miso you use in the dressing is a matter of personal preference. Experiment and see which one you prefer – they all contain subtle differences.

2 tablespoons dried *wakame* (see page 15), soaked in warm water
  for 5 minutes
2 x 150g (5oz) cod fillets
sweet *miso* dressing (see page 35)
125g (4¹/₂oz) rice
a little vegetable oil
¹/₂ teaspoon black sesame seeds

Drain the *wakame*, squeeze gently and roughly chop. Set aside.

Put the cod in a shallow bowl and pour over the sweet *miso* dressing. Leave in the fridge for 1 hour or overnight if possible. Cook the rice in a large pan of boiling water until tender, drain and keep warm.

Heat a griddle until hot and lightly oil with kitchen paper dipped in vegetable oil. Put the cod fillets on the griddle and cook, skin-side down, for 5 minutes. Turn over and cook for a further 2 minutes, or until opaque right through. The *miso* should be coloured, but not black.

Divide the rice between 2 plates and sprinkle over the black sesame seeds. Put the seaweed on top and finally the *miso* cod.

Bench seating and communal tables are hallmarks of wagamama. They make for a bustling, exciting atmosphere and lots of exchange. Regulars help newcomers and it allows groups to shrink and grow with ease.

kai sen udon

stir fried seafood with oyster sauce and udon noodles

You can vary the seafood used here, but the shapes are half the fun; squid, prawns and scallops all lending their own texture and flavour wrapped up in a broth heady with the flavours of soy and sesame oil, garlic and oyster sauce.

400g (14oz) *udon* noodles
2 teaspoons cornflour
2 tablespoons vegetable oil
2 garlic cloves, peeled and crushed
1 red pepper, trimmed and very thinly sliced
12 baby squid, cleaned
4 uncooked peeled prawns
8 queen scallops
12 slices of *chikuwa* (see page 14)
2 tablespoons *shaoshing* wine (see page 15)
150ml (¼ pint) water
1 teaspoon salt
1 teaspoon sugar
2 tablepoons oyster sauce
1 tablespoon light soy sauce
50g (2oz) pak choi, roughly chopped
2 teaspoons sesame oil
1 crabstick, shredded
large pinch of crushed black pepper

Cook the noodles in a large pan of boiling water for 2–3 minutes until just tender. Drain thoroughly, refresh under cold water and set aside. Mix 2 tablespoons cold water with the cornflour.

Heat a wok over a medium heat for 1–2 minutes or until completely hot and almost smoking and add the vegetable oil. Stir fry the garlic for 5 seconds, being careful not to let it brown. Add the red pepper and stir fry for 1 minute, then add the seafood and stir fry for 30 seconds. Pour in the wine and water and quickly bring to the boil. Add the salt, sugar, oyster sauce and soy sauce. Add the pak choi, then the cornflour paste and bring back to the boil – the sauce should have a coating consistency. Stir through the sesame oil.

Divide the noodles between 2 plates and top with the contents of the wok. Top with the shredded crabstick and crushed black pepper.

Pak choi is widely used in dishes throughout this book. Like spinach, its leaves melt to a silky texture, but the stems add crunch and body. It keeps well in the fridge for 2–3 days.

smoked haddock ramen

with chives and baby vegetables

225g (8oz) smoked haddock
1 tablespoon finely chopped Chinese chives (regular chives can be used,
    though they lack the garlic kick of Chinese chives)
large pinch of black pepper
250g (9oz) *ramen* noodles
1 litre (1¾ pints) *miso* soup (see page 46)
50g (2oz) baby sweetcorn
50g (2oz) courgettes
large handful of watercress
25g (1oz) *konbu* (see page 14), soaked in warm water for
    5 minutes and drained
12 pieces *menma* (canned bamboo shoots), drained

Put the haddock, skin-side down, in a pan. Cover with water, put on the lid, bring to the boil and simmer for 5 minutes or until opaque right through. Gently flake the fish, removing any bones and skin, and discard the liquor. Add the Chinese chives and black pepper.

Cook the noodles in a large pan of boiling water for 2–3 minutes until just tender. Drain thoroughly, refresh under cold water and divide between 2 bowls. Heat the *miso* soup until boiling, then add the baby vegetables and cook for 3 minutes, or until tender. Ladle the soup and vegetables over the noodles and top with the watercress and haddock, *konbu* and *menma*.

smoked fish should be a dusty, elegant colour, not strong and vivid. If you encounter the latter it has probably been dyed. There is little reason for this beyond a perception that some customers prefer it. The colour is hardly attractive and what is the point?

It really does make sense to assemble all the ingredients for a recipe before you start. The cooking process is not helped if you are rushing around trying to find something while your wok catches fire! Take time over the preparation and all will follow in one seamless stream.

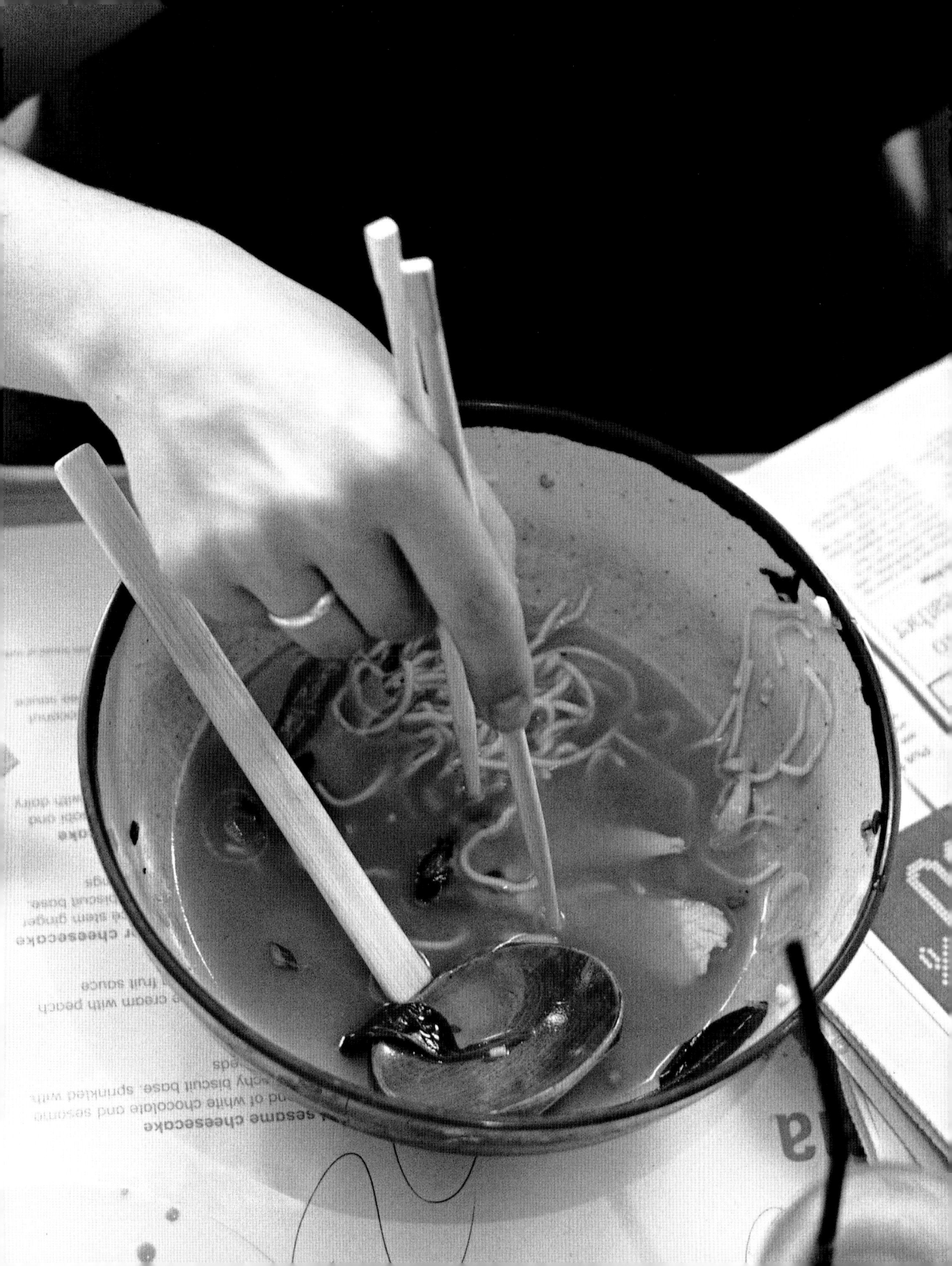

suzuki amiyaki soba

sea bass, pak choi, sesame oil and coriander

175g (6oz) cooked *soba* noodles

2 tablespoons vegetable oil

1 red onion, peeled and thinly sliced

2 baby pak choi, trimmed and stems sliced

large handful of beansprouts

2 garlic cloves, peeled and finely chopped

2 teaspoons sesame oil

2 tablespoons *yasai soba* salad dressing (see page 39)

2 x 150g (5oz) sea bass fillets

salt and white pepper

1 tablespoon finely chopped shallots

2 sprigs of coriander

1 lime, cut into wedges, to serve

Cook the noodles in a large pan of boiling water for 2–3 minutes until just tender. Drain thoroughly and refresh under cold running water.

Heat a wok or heavy-bottomed frying pan over a medium heat for 1–2 minutes or until completely hot and almost smoking and add 1 tablespoon of the vegetable oil. Add the red onion, pak choi, beansprouts and garlic and stir fry for 1 minute until just warmed through, moving the vegetables around constantly so that the garlic does not burn. Remove from the heat.

Toss the noodles with the vegetables, sesame oil and the *yasai soba* salad dressing in a large bowl until thoroughly combined and cover with a tea towel.

Season the sea bass fillets with salt and pepper. Heat a heavy-bottomed frying pan and add the remaining vegetable oil. Add the fish, skin-side down, and cook for 2–3 minutes until almost opaque. Turn over and cook for a further minute.

Divide the noodles and vegetables between 2 bowls and top with the sea bass. Sprinkle with the shallots and coriander and serve with lime wedges.

Previous spread, right: If you can use chopsticks that's all well and good, but we provide cutlery for anyone shy of trying. All the staff will happily show you, however, and those paper placemats are ideal for covering up any early mistakes.

hake tempura

deep-fried hake with ramen noodles, watercress and chilli

There is nothing difficult about making tempura dishes; just make sure you use ice-cold lager and pure vegetable oil and don't over-whisk the batter mixture. That way, it will remain light and airy rather than gooey and elastic.

½ egg, beaten
125ml (4fl oz) cold lager
pinch of bicarbonate of soda
salt and white pepper
50g (2oz) plain flour, plus extra for dusting
400ml (14fl oz) vegetable oil
400g (14oz) hake, skinned and cut into 8 large chunks
300g (10½oz) *ramen* noodles
1 litre/1¾ pints vegetable stock (see page 18)
small handful of watercress
handful of beansprouts
6 spring onions, trimmed and cut on the diagonal into 2.5cm (1in) slices
1 red chilli, trimmed and sliced

Cook the noodles in a large pan of boiling water for 2–3 minutes until just tender. Drain thoroughly, refresh under cold water and divide between 2 bowls.

Combine the egg, lager, bicarbonate of soda, a seasoning of salt and pepper and the flour in a bowl and whisk to form a light batter. Heat the oil in a heavy-bottomed saucepan until a little batter dropped in sinks to the bottom and then rises up. (If the batter stays down, the oil is not hot enough.)

Dip the fish in the extra flour and then in the batter and deep fry 4 pieces at a time for 5 minutes until golden and cooked through. Make sure that none sticks to the bottom of the pan, which can happen if the oil is not quite hot enough.

Bring the vegetable stock to the boil and ladle over the noodles. Top with the watercress and beansprouts. Put the fish pieces on top and sprinkle with the slices of spring onion and chilli.

salmon ramen

teriyaki salmon with baby vegetables, miso soup and noodles

250g (9oz) *ramen* noodles

50g (2oz) baby vegetables (sweetcorn, sugarsnaps or mangetout)
   or pak choi

a little vegetable oil

2 x 150g (5oz) salmon fillets

2 tablespoons teriyaki sauce, homemade (see page 28) or bought

1 litre (1¾ pints) chicken or vegetable stock (see pages 17 and 18)

75g (3oz) *miso* paste (see page 19)

12 pieces *menma* (canned bamboo shoots), drained

4 spring onions, trimmed and finely sliced

Cook the noodles in a large pan of boiling water for 2–3 minutes until just tender. Add the baby vegetables or pak choi for the final 2 minutes to cook until just tender. Drain and refresh everything under cold running water.

Heat a heavy-bottomed frying pan or griddle until hot, lightly oil with kitchen paper dipped in vegetable oil and cook the salmon for 2 minutes on each side, or until opaque right through. Warm the teriyaki sauce in a small pan and brush to coat the salmon.

Bring the stock to the boil in a large pan, then whisk in the *miso* paste until smooth. Divide the noodles and vegetables between 2 bowls and ladle over the stock. Top with the salmon, *menma* and spring onion slices.

Oodles of noodles: they are absolutely central to wagamama. Typically the restaurants serve over 6,000kg (12,000lb) of ramen noodles in a week.

sake amiyaki gohan

grilled salmon with pak choi, ginger, oyster sauce and steamed rice

2 x 150g (5oz) salmon fillets

2 teaspoons vegetable oil

1 garlic clove, peeled, finely chopped and crushed with a little salt

1 tablespoon peeled and grated fresh ginger root

1 small red onion, peeled and cut into chunks

1 red chilli, trimmed and thinly sliced

2 heads of pak choi, halved lengthways

500ml (18fl oz) boiling water

1 tablespoon oyster sauce

2 teaspoons light soy sauce

1 teaspoon salt

1 tablespoon sugar

14 mangetout

1 tablespoon *shaoshing* wine (see page 15)

1 tablespoon sesame oil

1 teaspoon cornflour

steamed Japanese rice, to serve

Preheat the grill. Put the salmon on a lightly oiled baking tray, skin-side down, and grill for 2 minutes, then turn over and cook for a further 6 minutes.

Heat a wok or large frying pan over a medium heat for 1–2 minutes or until completely hot and almost smoking and add the vegetable oil. Stir fry the garlic and ginger for 5 seconds, taking care not to let them colour too much. Add the onion, chilli and pak choi and stir fry for a further 30 seconds. Pour in the water, oyster and soy sauces, and add the salt and sugar. Bring to the boil. Add the mangetout and cook for 1 minute. Splash in the wine and sesame oil.

Mix the cornflour to a paste with a little cold water. Remove 2 tablespoons of the sauce from the wok and combine with the paste. Return to the wok and stir over a medium heat for 5 minutes or until you have a shiny sauce.

Place a portion of rice on 2 plates and top with the salmon. Pour over the sauce from the wok.

The skin on fish is too often discarded. Seasoned and cooked correctly so it crisps up, it provides both a textural and flavour contrast, as well as dramatic colour variation.

salmon korroke

salmon cakes with amai sauce, mixed leaves and wakame

makes 6 cakes

7 tablepoons vegetable oil

1 onion, peeled and finely chopped

1 small carrot, peeled and finely chopped

25g (1oz) frozen peas

200g (7oz) floury potatoes, peeled
   and quartered

300g (10½oz) salmon fillet

25g (1oz) canned sweetcorn, drained

salt and white pepper

3 eggs

4 heaped tablespoons plain flour

50g (2oz) *panko* breadcrumbs (see page 15)

2 tablespoons *amai* sauce (see page 22)

2 tablespoons wagamama salad dressing (see page 32)

2 large handfuls of mixed salad leaves

50g (2oz) *wakame*, soaked in warm water for 5 minutes, to garnish

The secret to a really good fishcake is to ensure the fish remains the key focus. That and a light hand in the forming. The idea is to keep the texture elegant and fluffy and allow the flavour of the fish to come through. Success is all in the detail.

Heat a wok over a medium heat for 1–2 minutes until hot and almost smoking and add 2 tablespoons of the oil. Add the onion, cover and cook over a very low heat for 5 minutes until translucent, stirring to make sure it doesn't catch and colour. Add the carrot and cook for a further 5 minutes; add the peas for the last minute.

Put the potatoes in cold water, cover, bring to the boil and cook for 10 minutes. Add the salmon and cook for 7 minutes until it is cooked right through and the potatoes are tender. Lift out the salmon and flake. Drain the potatoes, return to the pan and mash.

Combine the salmon and potatoes in a bowl along with the onion mixture and the sweetcorn. Season thoroughly and add 2 of the eggs. Beat into the mixture and combine thoroughly. Divide into 6 equal portions and shape into fishcakes.

Put the flour in one bowl, the remaining egg, beaten, in another and the breadcrumbs in a third. Dip the salmon cakes first in the flour, then in the egg and finally in the crumbs.

Heat a large frying pan, then add the remaining oil. Fry the fishcakes over a medium-low heat for 2–3 minutes on each side until golden. Drain on kitchen paper. Heat the *amai* sauce. Divide the salmon cakes between 2 plates and drizzle the sauce around the plates.

Mix the dressing with the salad leaves and place small mounds on top of the salmon cakes. Garnish with *wakame*.

salmon hot pot

with carrot, leek, soy sauce and brown rice

This is one of the few dishes in the book that doesn't feature on the wagamama menu, but works beautifully in the home setting where 30 minutes cooking time isn't a problem.

400g (14oz) salmon
2 tablespoons vegetable oil
1 leek, trimmed and finely sliced
1 tablespoon finely chopped shallot
1 carrot, peeled and finely diced
1 stick celery, peeled of any strings and finely diced
1 teaspoon sugar
2 garlic cloves, peeled and finely chopped
salt and white pepper
75ml (3fl oz) light soy sauce
300g (10½oz) cooked brown rice

Preheat the oven to 180°C/350°F/Gas 4. Remove any skin and bones from the salmon and cut the flesh into bite-sized pieces. Heat the oil in a flameproof casserole and when it is hot add the leek, shallot, carrot and celery and sauté gently for 10 minutes. Add the sugar and garlic, cook for a further minute and then add the fish and season with salt and pepper. Pour over the soy sauce, add 4 tablespoons water, cover and bake in the oven for 15 minutes. Remove and allow to rest for 5 minutes. Divide the rice between 2 bowls and ladle over the salmon hot pot.

Chefs go through a lot of training when they start. Many are new to kitchens, or have worked in places where systems are not important. For wagamama quality is our first priority and we must deliver that consistently well. Every dish has a procedure to follow, so each time it comes out looking and tasting equally good.

spiced sake soba

salmon soba with oyster mushrooms and red and yellow peppers

225g (8oz) *soba* noodles
2 tablespoons vegetable oil
2 x 150g (5oz) salmon fillets
salt
½ yellow pepper, trimmed, deseeded and sliced
½ red pepper, trimmed, deseeded and sliced
½ red onion, peeled and sliced
handful of oyster mushrooms
large handful of beansprouts
1 courgette, cut into thin strips
1 tablespoon rice vinegar
2 tablespoons chilli oil (see page 19)
1 tablespoon fried onions
2 tablespoons *yaki soba* sauce (see page 32)
2 eggs, beaten
1 teaspoon sesame seeds
1 lemon, cut into wedges, to serve

Cook the noodles in a large pan of boiling water for 2–3 minutes until just tender. Drain and refresh under cold running water. Heat a frying pan until hot and add 1 tablespoon of the vegetable oil. Season the skin on the salmon with salt, then cook, skin-side down, over a high heat for 5 minutes, turn over and cook for 2 minutes. Set aside.

Meanwhile, heat a wok or large frying pan over a medium heat for 1–2 minutes or until completely hot and almost smoking and add the remaining vegetable oil. Add the peppers, onion, mushrooms, beansprouts, courgette, rice vinegar, chilli oil and the fried onions. Stir fry for 5–8 minutes until tender. Stir in the noodles and *yaki soba* sauce and cook for 1–2 minutes.

Add the eggs and stir fry for a further minute or until the eggs are cooked. Divide between 2 dishes, scatter over the sesame seeds and top with the salmon fillet and a lemon wedge.

our website is a central part of our communications strategy. Talk to us and we will talk to you. We fundamentally believe in listening and responding to you. For us the customer really does come first.

yaki soba

stir fried chicken and prawns with soba noodles and pickled ginger

This dish has become known as *yaki soba* even though, traditionally, it doesn't use *soba* noodles. You can use *ramen* instead if you prefer, as we do in the restaurants.

110g (4oz) *soba* noodles
2 tablespoons *yaki soba* sauce (see page 32)
1 small onion, peeled and cut into half-moon slices
4 spring onions, trimmed and cut into 2.5cm (1in) lengths
large handful of beansprouts
15 small cooked peeled prawns
2 tablespoons vegetable oil
1 boneless, skinless chicken breast, cut into strips
½ red pepper, trimmed, deseeded and cubed
½ green pepper, trimmed, deseeded and cubed
2 eggs, beaten

to serve
25g (1oz) pickled ginger (*gari*, see page 14)
1 tablespoon dried shallots
½ teaspoon toasted sesame seeds (see page 164)

Cook the noodles in a large pan of boiling water for 2–3 minutes until just tender. Drain and refresh under cold running water.

Put the *yaki soba* sauce, the onion, spring onion, beansprouts and prawns in a large bowl and mix in the noodles.

Heat a wok over a medium heat for 1–2 minutes or until completely hot and almost smoking and add the vegetable oil. Add the chicken and red and green peppers and stir fry for 2 minutes. Add the noodles and vegetables to the wok and stir fry quickly for 3 minutes until warmed through. Add the eggs and continue to stir fry for a further minute or until the eggs are just cooked. Serve with the pickled ginger, shallots and sesame seeds.

A wok with one long handle is easier to toss and that is what's so crucial to stir frying because it keeps the ingredients moving constantly round the pan. The flicking of the wrist is almost impossible with two handles but then some people prefer to stir and there is nothing wrong with that.

in Japan there are four main types of noodles: *ramen* (Chinese style), *soba* (wholemeal), *udon* (thick and white) and *somen* (thin and white). Does it matter which one you use? Not really, but as with pasta, spaghetti Bolognese just isn't the same if you don't use spaghetti.

monkfish yakitori

with green-tea soba noodles, soy, ginger and lime

Monkfish is perfect at picking up strong flavours and is a dream to grill. If you want a variation on this recipe try using scallops, which are even more succulent. If you cannot find lemongrass stalks, wooden skewers make perfectly good substitutes.

4 spring onions, trimmed and cut into 4cm (1½in) lengths

300g (10½oz) monkfish, cleaned, boned and cut into 2.5cm (1in) slices

2 lemongrass stalks, outer leaves removed, split lengthways

1 tablespoon vegetable oil

salt and white pepper

250g (9oz) *soba* noodles

400ml (14fl oz) green tea

generous handful of roughly chopped choi sum (see page 14)

generous handful of beansprouts

1 garlic clove, peeled and crushed

1 green chilli, trimmed and sliced

1 teaspoon chopped coriander

1 red onion, peeled and finely sliced

for the dressing

1 tablespoon olive oil

2 tablespoons light soy sauce

½ teaspoon peeled and grated fresh ginger root

juice of 1 lime

½ teaspoon sugar

These yakitori make fantastic party food when served on their own. Just the thing to partner ice-cold beers.

Preheat the grill. Make a small slit in each cut length of spring onion. Thread the monkfish and spring onion pieces equally onto the 2 lemongrass stalks. Place on a baking tray and brush with the vegetable oil. Season with salt and pepper.

Place the tray of monkfish *yakitori* under the hot grill and cook for 6–7 minutes, turning the stalks once.

Meanwhile, cook the noodles in a large pan of boiling hot green tea for 2–3 minutes until just tender. Drain thoroughly and refresh under cold running water. Combine the remaining ingredients, toss with the noodles in a large bowl and divide between 2 plates.

Top the noodle mixture with the monkfish. Mix together all the dressing ingredients and drizzle over.

seafood ramen

with menma, mangetout, noodles and spring onions

Seafood *ramen* is another top seller, the perfect fast food offering a nutritionally complete meal in a bowl. One-stop dining of the best kind and able to provide you with energy that you will start to burn immediately.

250g (9oz) *ramen* noodles

1 litre (1¾ pints) chicken or vegetable stock (see pages 17 and 18)

50g (2oz) mangetout and baby sweetcorn

10 small squid, prepared

4 cooked tiger prawns, peeled and deveined

2 crabsticks

2 x 5mm (¼in) slices *kamaboko-aka* (see page 14)

12 pieces *menma* (canned bamboo shoots), drained

25g (1oz) *wakame* (see page 15), soaked in warm water for
   5 minutes and roughly sliced

4 spring onions, trimmed and finely sliced

Cook the noodles in a large pan of boiling water for 2–3 minutes until tender. Drain thoroughly and refresh under cold running water.

Bring the stock to the boil in a large pan. Add the mangetout and baby corn and cook for 3 minutes until just tender. Add the squid, cook for 1 minute, then add the prawns and remove the pan from the heat.

Divide the noodles between 2 bowls and ladle over the stock, vegetables and fish. Top with the crabsticks, *kamaboko-aka*, *menma*, *wakame* and spring onions.

Food this good, this fast? Until I tasted a bowl of your chicken ramen I thought all fast food was rubbish. Thanks for breaking the mould.
Francoise, Paris

mackerel with soy and ginger

with sake, mirin and Japanese rice

1 mackerel, scaled, cleaned and filleted

for the marinade

3 tablespoons light soy sauce

2.5cm (1in) piece of fresh ginger root, peeled and grated

1 garlic clove, peeled, chopped and mashed to a paste with a little salt

2 tablespoons sake

1 tablespoon *mirin* (see page 14)

1 teaspoon sugar

to serve

300g (10½oz) cooked Japanese short-grain rice

pickles (see page 15)

Place the fish fillets, skin-side down, in a flat china dish or non-metallic container. Mix together all the marinade ingredients and spoon over the fish. Set aside for 1 hour.

Preheat the grill, then cook the marinated fillets, skin-side down, for 2 minutes. Turn over, brush with extra marinade and grill for a further 3–4 minutes or until the skin is well blistered and golden.

Divide the rice between 2 plates, top with a fillet of mackerel each and serve with a portion of pickles.

We don't stand on ceremony in the restaurants. You cannot book a table, no smoking is allowed and your order is keyed into a hand-held computer. That way you get to sit down quickly and your food can arrive in moments. Wagamama was conceived as a non-destinational food station. It is designed to be easy and accessible.

6

meat

At the heart of wagamama lies a culinary holy trinity: a bowl of noodles, the soup or broth base, and a topping. When founder Alan Yau was working on the original scheme for the first restaurant in Streatham Street in London's Bloomsbury, it was essentially this dish – eaten at noodle stalls throughout the Far East but particularly in Tokyo – he saw at the core of the menu. It has remained there ever since.

In Tokyo these stalls are very simple affairs: a bench and a few pots holding the hot stock, the noodles and the various toppings. Good food prepared fast – exactly what many of us want at home. Unlike many so-called fast-food restaurants, the huge benefit of this way of cooking is that the quality is high and it remains healthy. At wagamama we spend a great deal of time and attention sourcing prime ingredients and doing as little to them as possible. We might marinate meat to enhance its flavour, but apart from that the inherent qualities of the dish come from the other ingredients added – a little chilli perhaps, lemongrass, red peppers or finely sliced spring onion.

When you try these recipes at home, the time for marinating the meat may be short, but don't let that put you off. Half an hour will make a substantial difference. The dish won't taste quite the same, or have the same depth of flavour, but it will still be delicious.

You might be surprised to see how little meat is used in the following recipes. This is very much in keeping with the whole noodle philosophy and not that far from the Italian view on meat in pasta dishes: a little goes a long way. With our increasing awareness of the need for healthier eating, the idea of less, but better quality, is central to our thinking.

Quality and consistency are what wagamama is all about. As we have expanded, consistency has come to play a major role – it has to. Driving that knowledge back into the company is aimed at one key target: maintaining and improving quality. This same attention to detail is carried through in these recipes. Restaurant recipes (we call them specs) seldom automatically transfer to a domestic setting, so we have developed and tested each one in a domestic kitchen to ensure they work properly.

Kaizen is the Japanese word for gradual, ongoing and simple improvements. In essence it means you do things, learn things, then you do more things. Never standing still may be a more straightforward explanation but that suggests a random approach. Cooking is so much about confidence and that can only be attained by doing, learning and then moving on.

Although the list of ingredients in some of these recipes may seem long, many of them will be – or can be – in your store cupboard. A bowl of noodles today, *teppanyaki* tomorrow.

shichimi spiced duck ramen

noodle soup with spring greens

2 x 150g (5oz) boneless duck breasts (skin on)

2 teaspoons *shichimi* (see page 15)

½ teaspoon salt

½ teaspoon sugar

250g (9oz) *ramen* noodles

1 litre (1¾ pints) vegetable stock (see page 18)

2 handfuls of roughly chopped pak choi or baby spinach

4 spring onions, trimmed and finely sliced

Prepare the duck by lightly scoring the skin. Mix the *shichimi*, salt and sugar together in a shallow dish and lay the duck breasts in the marinade, skin-side down. Put a plate on top and weigh it down with something heavy – say a couple of unopened cans of baked beans. Place the weighted duck in the fridge and marinate for 1 hour or if possible overnight.

To cook the duck, preheat a griddle or frying pan over a medium heat for 1–2 minutes until hot and almost smoking. Cook the duck, skin-side down, for 5 minutes, then turn over and cook on the other side for 3 minutes or until cooked. Set aside to rest for 5 minutes.

To serve, cook the noodles in a large pan of boiling water for 2–3 minutes or until just tender. Drain and divide between 2 bowls. Bring the vegetable stock to the boil, add the pak choi and cook for 1 minute, then ladle over the noodles. Check the seasoning. Thinly slice the duck at a slight angle and place on top along with the spring onions.

Far left: The recipes in this book contain a lot of chopping and a sharp knife is essential. You can spend a great deal of money on one (up-market kitchen shops), or not very much at all (ethnic supermarkets and simply replace often), depending on your budget. Left: Noodles ready to go. Cooking them ahead of finally composing the dish really does make life a lot easier.

chilli beef ramen

with beansprouts, red onion and lime

150g (5oz) beansprouts
250g (9oz) *ramen* noodles
350g (12oz) sirloin steak, 2cm (¾in) thick, in the piece
a little vegetable oil
a little teriyaki sauce, for brushing
1 litre (1¾ pints) chicken or vegetable stock (see page 17)
2 tablespoons chilli *ramen* sauce (see page 23)
4 spring onions, trimmed and sliced
1 red chilli, trimmed, deseeded and sliced lengthways
½ red onion, peeled and very thinly sliced
1 lime, quartered
6 sprigs of coriander

Blanch the beansprouts in a large pan of boiling water for 10 seconds. Drain, reserving the water, and refresh in cold running water. Cook the noodles in the reserved boiling water for 2–3 minutes or until just tender. Drain thoroughly and refresh under cold running water.

Heat a griddle or frying pan over a medium heat for 1–2 minutes until hot and almost smoking. Lightly rub the steak with oil, then cook for 2 minutes on each side until medium rare. Remove from the griddle, brush with the teriyaki sauce and keep warm while it rests for 3–4 minutes. Slice on the diagonal.

Divide the noodles between 2 bowls. Heat the stock, stir in the chilli *ramen* sauce, then ladle over the noodles. Top with the beef, beansprouts, spring onions, chilli, red onion, 2 lime quarters and the coriander.

It's in the bowl. Ramen continues to be one of our top sellers, a complete meal in one; fast and nutritious; simple food at its best.

chillies are one of those ingredients about which people tend to feel strongly. Love them or hate them, what is wonderful is how easy it is to include them or leave them out. In the restaurants we tend to use them sparsely – people can always ask for more or add chilli sauce if they want that extra kick. But at home, you can do what you want.

pork and beef cabbage rolls

with spring onion, chilli and soy sauce

8 large Chinese cabbage outer leaves

salt and black pepper

50g (2oz) lean minced pork

50g (2oz) lean minced beef

1 small onion, peeled and chopped

4 spring onions, trimmed and chopped

1 green chilli, trimmed, deseeded and finely chopped

50g (2oz) cooked Japanese rice

4 cocktail sticks

for the stock

1 tablespoon *mirin* (see page 14)

600ml (1 pint) *dashi*, made with *dashi no moto* (see page 14)

1 tablespoon light soy sauce

1 tablespoon sake

Cook the cabbage leaves in a large pan of lightly salted boiling water for 3 minutes. Drain and lay flat on a clean tea towel to cool. Cut a triangle out of the thickest end of the stems (you can leave some stem) and discard. In a large bowl combine the minced pork and beef, onion, spring onions and chilli. Lightly season with salt and black pepper, then add the cooked rice and mix to bind everything together.

Overlap 2 cabbage leaves on a chopping board, place a quarter of the meat filling in the centre and fold up the leaves to form a parcel. Secure with a cocktail stick. Prepare three other parcels in the same way.

Bring the *mirin, dashi*, soy sauce, sake and a pinch of salt to the boil, then lower the heat to a simmer. Add the cabbage parcels and cover with a lid. Simmer for 40 minutes or until the meat is cooked. To serve, lift out of the stock, remove the cocktail sticks and slice in half. Place in 2 serving bowls and ladle over some of the stock.

These parcels also make fantastic canapes. You can make the stuffed parcels in advance but stop before you cook them because the cabbage tends to discolour an hour or so after it is cooked.

pork belly hot pot

with mixed vegetables, sake and miso

50g (2oz) *konnyaku*, (see page 14), optional

3 tablespoons vegetable oil

150g (5oz) belly pork, cut into thin strips (alternatively use streaky bacon)

1 red onion, peeled and sliced

110g (4oz) *daikon* (mooli), peeled and shredded

2 carrots, peeled and grated

110g (4oz) sweet potato, peeled and julienned

4 shiitake mushrooms

8 baby sweetcorn, halved lengthways

400ml (14fl oz) *dashi*, made with *dashi no moto* (see page 14)

1 tablespoon sake

25g (1oz) *miso* paste (see page 19)

If using *konnyaku*, place in a small pan and cover with water. Bring to the boil over a moderate heat, then drain and allow to cool. Roughly chop the *konnyaku*.

Heat a wok over a medium heat for 1–2 minutes or until completely hot and almost smoking and add the vegetable oil. Add the pork and stir fry for 1 minute. Add the vegetables and stir fry for a further minute. Pour in the *dashi* and sake, bring to the boil and simmer for 10 minutes.

Remove 2 tablespoons of stock from the wok and blend with the *miso* paste to dissolve it. Pour the mixture back into the pan and cook for a further minute. Divide between 2 bowls.

*Fast and friendly service...
Delicious food... And the
waiters are a gorgeous
bunch of blokes too!*
Anjin, Norway

roasted honey pork ramen

with seasonal greens, bamboo shoots and barbecue sauce

Steaming broth, sweetened roasted pork and lots of interesting greens to complete one of our popular specials. This dish is particularly sought after in the colder months, when big, gutsy flavours are required.

275g (10oz) pork fillet

2 tablespoons barbecue sauce (see page 29)

2 teaspoons runny honey

275g (10oz) *ramen* noodles

1 litre (1¾ pints) seasoned chicken stock (see page 17)

4 spring onions, trimmed and cut into 2.5cm (1in) lengths

2 handfuls of roughly chopped seasonal greens

12 pieces *menma* (canned bamboo shoots), drained

Preheat the oven to 220°C/425°F/Gas 7. Put the pork in a roasting tray, add the barbecue sauce and toss to coat. Roast for approximately 30 minutes. After 25 minutes, pour over the honey and return to the oven for the final 5 minutes. Leave to rest for 5 minutes, then slice thinly.

Cook the noodles in a large pan of boiling water for 2–3 minutes until just tender. Drain thoroughly and divide between 2 bowls. Heat the chicken stock until boiling, add the spring onions and greens and cook for 30 seconds.

Ladle over the noodles. Top with the *menma* and the pork.

When you order your choice is keyed into an electronic pad, which sends the selection through to the kitchen. This means your food is often being prepared before you have even had time to settle down.

pork char siu men

five-spice roast pork with pak choi and noodles

300g (10½oz) pork fillet

2 tablespoons vegetable oil

250g (9oz) *ramen* noodles

75g (3oz) pak choi or baby vegetables

1 litre (1¾ pints) chicken stock (see page 17)

12 pieces *menma* (canned bamboo shoots), drained

4 spring onions, trimmed and chopped

for the marinade

1 tablespoon *char siu* sauce (see page 14)

½ teaspoon Chinese five spice (available from Oriental stores)

¼ teaspoon ground cinnamon

2 tablespoons sake

Put the pork and the marinade ingredients in a polythene freezer bag, massage for a few minutes and transfer to the fridge overnight or for as long as possible.

Preheat the oven to 150°C/300°F/Gas 2. Heat a heavy-bottomed frying pan until hot, add the vegetable oil and put the pork in for 2–3 minutes to seal, rolling it around until golden all over. Transfer to a roasting tray and roast for 50 minutes–1 hour. Remove and rest for 5 minutes, then slice on the diagonal.

Cook the noodles in a large pan of boiling water for 2–3 minutes or until just tender. Drain thoroughly and refresh under cold running water.

Steam or boil the pak choi for 1 minute or vegetables for 5 minutes until just tender. Put the stock in a pan and bring to the boil. Divide the noodles between 2 bowls and ladle over the stock. Top with the slices of pork and pak choi, *menma* and spring onions.

tonkatsu

golden breadcrumbed pork with chilli, daikon and mangetout

The *katsu* dishes are popular sellers on the menu; it's something about those crispy breadcrumbs. The recipe for *tonkatsu* comes from the Amsterdam wagamama where it has proved a popular dish from the day it appeared as a special.

2 carrots, peeled and julienned

50g (2oz) *daikon* (mooli), peeled and julienned

25g (1oz) mangetout, thinly sliced on the diagonal

8 spring onions, trimmed and thinly sliced on the diagonal

1 green chilli, trimmed, deseeded and sliced lengthways

handful of beansprouts, well rinsed

2 x 150g (5oz) pork loin steaks

flour, for dusting

1 egg, beaten

generous handful of *panko* breadcrumbs (see page 15)

4 tablespoons vegetable oil

2 handfuls of salad leaves

1 tablespoon tomato ketchup

2 tablespoons Worcestershire sauce

Put the carrots, *daikon*, mangetout, spring onions, chilli and beansprouts in iced water for 1 hour to crisp up. Drain thoroughly.

Place the pork between 2 sheets of clingfilm and bat out with a rolling pin until only 5mm (¼in) thick. Put the flour in one bowl, the egg in another and the breadcrumbs in a third. Dip the pork first in the flour, then in the egg and finally in the crumbs. Press gently to coat well.

Heat a heavy-bottomed frying pan over a medium heat for 1–2 minutes until hot and almost smoking and add the oil. Add the pork and cook for 3 minutes on each side until golden. Drain the pork on kitchen paper and cut into 1cm (½in) strips.

Divide between 2 plates, along with the drained vegetables, and arrange the salad leaves alongside. Combine the ketchup and Worcestershire sauce and pour around the pork.

lamb kare lomen

marinated lamb with soba noodles, coriander and teriyaki dipping sauce

200g (7oz) noisettes of lamb fillet

2 garlic cloves, peeled, chopped and mashed with a little salt

4 tablespoons vegetable oil

200ml (7fl oz) *kare lomen* sauce (see page 38)

½ teaspoon salt

½ teaspoon sugar

½ teaspoon *dashi no moto* (see page 14)

200ml (7fl oz) coconut milk

250g (9oz) thin white *somen* noodles

handful of beansprouts

small bunch of coriander, roughly chopped

75g (3oz) cucumber, julienned

to serve

1 tablespoon barbecue sauce (see page 29)

1 tablespoon teriyaki sauce, homemade (see page 28) or bought

2 lime wedges

Combine the lamb and garlic, toss well and set aside.

Heat a wok over a medium heat for 1–2 minutes or until completely hot and almost smoking and add the vegetable oil. Pour in the *kare lomen* sauce and simmer for 15 minutes, or until the sauce takes on a deep, dark red colour and gives off a sweet, rounded aroma. Add 250ml (9fl oz) water and bring to the boil, whisking all the time. Season with salt, sugar and *dashi no moto*. Add the coconut milk and simmer for 5 minutes.

Preheat the grill. Grill the lamb for 3 minutes, turn over and repeat on the other side until cooked. Set aside in a warm place to rest.

Cook the noodles in a large pan of boiling water for 2–3 minutes or until just tender. Drain thoroughly, then divide between 2 bowls.

Spoon over the hot *kare lomen* sauce and add the beansprouts, coriander and cucumber. Top with the lamb, spoon over a little of the barbecue sauce and teriyaki sauce and serve with the lime wedges.

zasai beef gohan

stir fried beef with red pepper, mushrooms, oyster sauce and rice

200g (7oz) rice

2 tablespoons vegetable oil

150g (5oz) rump or sirloin steak, cut on the diagonal
    into thin strips

2 garlic cloves, peeled and mashed with a little salt

handful of mangetout, thinly sliced

4 spring onions, trimmed and sliced

½ red pepper, trimmed, deseeded and cut into thin strips

8 baby sweetcorn, sliced

6 shiitake mushrooms, sliced

1 tablespoon *shaoshing* wine (see page 15)

pinch of salt

1 teaspoon white sugar

2 tablespoons light soy sauce

1 tablespoon oyster sauce

1 tablespoon sesame oil

3 tablespoons *zasai* chilli sauce (see page 36)

Cook the rice in a large pan of boiling water and drain. Heat a wok over a medium heat for 1–2 minutes or until completely hot and almost smoking and add the vegetable oil. Add the beef and garlic and stir fry for 30 seconds. Add the vegetables, wine, salt, sugar, soy sauce, oyster sauce and 75ml (3fl oz) water.

Mix the cornflour with 2 tablespoons of water and stir into the sauce. Bring to the boil, then stir in the sesame oil.

Divide the rice between 2 plates and top with the beef and the *zasai* chilli sauce.

Simple food places a great deal of emphasis on sourcing the best ingredients; the freshest vegetables, well-hung meat and mouthwatering sauces made alongside the main dish. Attention to detail drives all of what we do and this is equally important in a domestic kitchen.

7

vegetable
main dishes

On display in all wagamama kitchens is a chart simply headed 'How To Cut'. It lists all the vegetables we use and explains how to cut them. This level of detail is important for two reasons. First, as a restaurant group we must ensure consistency at a high standard. Second, how a dish looks is as essential to the Japanese as how it tastes and smells. Vision is, after all, one of our senses. So our team learns how to cut to ensure variety in a dish. Thus a pepper is cut in one of three ways – into chunks, batons or juliennes; a spring onion is either thinly sliced or long-sliced; a carrot is shredded or sliced to create rounds.

There is, of course, another constraining factor: all the ingredients in the restaurant dishes (and in recipes here) can be eaten with chopsticks. That means they need to be bite-sized and while this requirement limits the presentation, it also provides an enormously rewarding challenge.

It is impossible to discuss vegetables in Japanese cooking and not raise the subject of tofu, an ingredient people in the West have been slow to adopt. Tofu is rich in protein, the main reason for its popularity in countries where protein sources were scarce (in Japan, for example, the eating of meat is relatively recent).

Put simply, tofu is the milk of soya beans, which is coagulated to make it solid – bean curd. It doesn't have a great deal of taste itself, but it readily absorbs the flavours of other stronger-tasting ingredients. In this it is not that different from modern chicken, which is quite mild-tasting and is often 'improved' by being cooked with more strongly flavoured ingredients.

Sourcing good vegetables is no easy task and at wagamama we face the same problems as the home cook, albeit on a different scale. We insist on the freshest pak choi, spring onions and salad leaves. We go to great lengths to ensure our onions deliver punch without bitterness. We continuously strive to find cucumbers with crunch, carrots with bite, mushrooms with flavour.

the organic question Customers often ask about the relative merits of organic. Our answer remains the same: you must taste and judge for yourselves. In our experience, organic can sometimes be better, but it is not a universal truth. Rather than pinning our flag to the organic mast we prefer to go in search of what is best. That way we can ensure we deliver the maximum flavour and texture on the plate or in the bowl.

moyashi soba

stir fried vegetables with sesame oil and soy sauce

250g (9oz) wholemeal *ramen* noodles
1 litre (1¾ pints) vegetable stock (see page 18)
2 tablespoons vegetable oil
2 garlic cloves, peeled and crushed
2 large courgettes, cut on the diagonal into 5mm (¼in) thick slices
2 small leeks, trimmed and finely sliced
15 button mushrooms, finely sliced
14 sugarsnap peas
handful of beansprouts
8 x 2.5cm (1in) cubes of firm tofu
1 teaspoon salt
2 teaspoons sugar
2 tablespoons light soy sauce
2 teaspoons sesame oil
4 spring onions, trimmed and cut into 2.5cm (1in) slices

Cook the noodles in a large pan of boiling water for 2–3 minutes or until just tender. Drain, refresh under cold running water and divide between 2 bowls. Bring the stock to the boil using the same pan and ladle over the noodles.

Meanwhile, heat a wok over a medium heat for 1–2 minutes or until completely hot and almost smoking and add the vegetable oil. Stir fry the garlic for 5 seconds, then add all the vegetables and tofu, but not the spring onions. Stir fry for 2–3 minutes until softened. Add the salt, sugar and soy sauce, then drizzle over the sesame oil. Divide between the bowls and top with the spring onion slices.

noodles are delicious, quick and easy. They are also a source of complex carbohydrates. *Soba* noodles, made from buckwheat, are particularly healthy, as buckwheat is said to thin the blood and is thought to be one explanation for the low rate of heart disease in Japan. A reason, if one is needed, to slurp away.

rice noodle soup

with grilled tofu steak, miso and choi sum

150g (5oz) rice noodles
2 x 250g (9oz) firm tofu, cut into 2 steaks
2 tablespoons *miso* paste (see page 19)
½ teaspoon *shichimi* (see page 15)
1 tablespoon vegetable oil
handful of roughly chopped choi sum (see page 14)
1 litre (1¾ pints) *miso* soup (see page 46) or vegetable stock (see page 18)
small handful of coriander

Soak the noodles in hot water for 2 minutes, drain, refresh under cold running water and divide between 2 bowls. Place the tofu steaks between sheets of kitchen paper and pat dry. Combine the *miso* paste and *shichimi* and spread over the top of each steak.

Heat a griddle until hot and oil lightly with kitchen paper dipped in vegetable oil. Place the tofu on the griddle, *miso*-side up, for 6–8 minutes or until the tofu is hot and the base is crispy. Remove the steaks and cook the choi sum on the griddle until just wilted. Bring the *miso* soup or stock to the boil and ladle over the noodles. Top with the choi sum and griddled tofu. Scatter with coriander.

Shopping for noodles is nothing like as difficult as it once was. Most super-markets now carry quite a range, although ethnic supermarkets tend to be more extensive both in terms of type and the brands they have. Is there much to tell between each brand? Not a great deal, the best idea is to try a few and find one you like.

yasai chilli men

stir fried chilli vegetables with tofu and soba noodles

250g (9oz) *soba* noodles
2 tablespoons vegetable oil
6 x 2cm (¾in) cubes, firm tofu
6 button mushrooms, sliced
handful of sugarsnap peas
1 courgette, cut on the diagonal into 5mm (¼in) slices
2 carrots, peeled and thinly sliced
2 tomatoes, quartered
300ml (½ pint) chilli sauce (see page 27)

Cook the noodles in a large pan of boiling water for 2–3 minutes or until just tender. Drain and refresh under cold running water. Heat a wok over a medium heat for 1–2 minutes or until completely hot and almost smoking and add the vegetable oil. Add the tofu and stir fry for about 5 minutes until golden. Add all the vegetables and stir fry for 3–4 minutes until they are tender. Pour in the chilli sauce and bring to the boil. Divide the noodles between 2 plates and top with the stir fry.

ginger chilli mushrooms

with soba noodles, spring onions and coriander

250g (9oz) *soba* noodles

3 tablespoons vegetable oil

1 red chilli, trimmed, deseeded and finely sliced

2 tablespoons peeled and grated fresh ginger root

4 oyster mushrooms, cut into 1cm (½in) slices

4 shiitake mushrooms, cut into 1cm (½in) slices

clump of enoki mushrooms, about the size of your fist, broken up

handful of roughly chopped choi sum (see page 14)

½ teaspoon salt

1 teaspoon sugar

generous handful of beansprouts

600ml (1 pint) *miso* soup (see page 46)

4 spring onions, trimmed and sliced

2 sprigs of coriander

Cook the noodles in a large pan of boiling water for 2–3 minutes or until just tender. Drain, refresh under cold running water and divide between 2 bowls. Heat a wok over a medium heat for 1–2 minutes or until completely hot and almost smoking and add the vegetable oil. Add the sliced red chilli and grated ginger and stir fry for 15–20 seconds, then add the oyster, shiitake and enoki mushrooms and the choi sum. Season with salt and sugar, and stir fry for 2–3 minutes.

Put the beansprouts on top of the noodles, spoon over the mushrooms, then ladle over the hot *miso* soup. Scatter with the spring onion slices and coriander.

You only stir fry once, so everything has to be chopped to fit in with the time frame. This can seem a chore when you've been 'cooking' for 20 minutes without turning the heat on, but it all happens in a flash at the end.

marinated vegetable ramen

with soy sauce, garlic and chilli

1 small aubergine, trimmed and sliced

vegetable oil

1 small sweet potato, peeled and sliced

4 medium mushrooms, halved

1 courgette, sliced

4 baby sweetcorn, halved lengthways

4 spring onions, trimmed and cut into 2.5cm (1in) slices

2 tablespoons light soy sauce

1 teaspoon finely chopped garlic

1 red chilli, trimmed, deseeded and finely chopped

250g (9oz) wholemeal *ramen* noodles

1 litre (1¾ pints) vegetable stock (see page 18)

Heat a griddle until smoking. Brush the aubergine slices with oil. Put all the other vegetables in a large bowl and toss with 3 tablespoons of the oil until everything is coated.

Cook the aubergine first, for 4 minutes on each side, or until tender. Then cook the sweet potato, mushrooms and courgette, all of which should take about 2–3 minutes on each side. Finally cook the sweetcorn and spring onions for 1 minute on each side.

Transfer to a bowl, drizzle over the soy sauce, garlic and chilli, toss and cover with clingfilm. (It is important to marinate the vegetables while they are hot so that they absorb the flavours. They will soften up further on cooling.) Set aside to marinate for at least 20 minutes.

Cook the noodles in a large pan of boiling water for 2–3 minutes or until just tender. Drain thoroughly and divide between 2 bowls. Bring the vegetable stock to the boil and check the vegetables; if they are still a little tough, cook in the stock until tender. Ladle the stock and vegetables over the noodles.

Chargrilled aubergine has a meatiness quite unlike any other vegetable; succulent, full-flavoured and packed with gutsy attitude. Who needs meat when a vegetable can deliver all this?

yasai korroke

vegetable cakes with amai sauce, mixed leaves and wakame

makes 6 cakes

1 large potato, peeled and cut into chunks

1 small sweet potato, peeled and cut into chunks

salt and white pepper

25g (1oz) frozen peas

25g (1oz) canned sweetcorn, drained

vegetable oil, for deep frying

1 small onion, peeled and finely chopped

1 red chilli, trimmed and finely chopped

3–4 tablespoons plain flour

1 egg, beaten

50g (2oz) *panko* breadcrumbs (see page 15)

2 tablespoons *amai* sauce (see page 22)

2 handfuls of salad leaves

2 tablespoons wagamama salad dressing (see page 32)

½ red pepper, trimmed, deseeded and cut into thin strips

50g (2oz) *wakame* (see page 15), soaked in warm water for
   5 minutes, drained and roughly chopped

Calling these vegetable cakes doesn't really do them justice. Light, delicate and remarkably full-flavoured, they deliver quite a punch along with the amai sauce.

Put the potato and sweet potato in a pan of boiling salted water and cook for 10–12 minutes until tender. Add the peas for the last 2 minutes. Drain, return to the pan, then crush slightly with a wooden spoon to create a lumpy mash. Stir in the sweetcorn.

Heat 2 tablespoons of the oil in a frying pan and cook the onion and chilli over a low heat for 6–8 minutes until soft. Combine the onion and chilli with the cooked ingredients in a large bowl, season and mix evenly. Allow to cool, divide into 6 equal portions and shape into flat cakes.

Place the flour in a bowl, the beaten egg in another and the breadcrumbs in a third. Dip each cake first in the flour, then in the egg and finally in the crumbs.

Fill a pan two-thirds full with oil and heat to 180°C/350°F, or until a cube of bread added to the oil browns in 30 seconds. Lower in the cakes, 3 at a time, and deep fry for 2–3 minutes until golden brown and crisp. Drain the cakes on kitchen paper and keep warm while you deep fry the remainder.

Arrange the vegetable cakes on 2 plates. Heat the *amai* sauce and drizzle around the plate. Mix the salad leaves with the dressing and place on top of the cakes. Top with red pepper strips and *wakame*.

pumpkin curry

with tofu, brown rice, baby spinach and coconut ginger sauce

3 tablespoons vegetable oil

1 small pumpkin, peeled, deseeded and cut into wedges

2 courgettes, cut into small chunks

6 button mushrooms, halved

4 baby sweetcorn

handful of sugarsnap peas

4 x 2.5cm (1in) cubes of firm tofu

200ml (7fl oz) coconut ginger sauce (see page 25)

100g (3½oz) brown rice

2 handfuls of baby spinach

handful of chopped coriander

Heat a wok over a medium heat for 1–2 minutes or until completely hot and almost smoking and add the vegetable oil. Add the pumpkin, courgettes, mushrooms, baby sweetcorn and sugarsnap peas and stir fry for 2 minutes. Add the tofu and the coconut ginger sauce, season with a little salt and continue cooking for a further 15–20 minutes, or until the pumpkin is tender. Cook the rice according to the instructions on the packet. Drain and divide between 2 plates. Scatter the baby spinach on the plate alongside and spoon over the curry. Sprinkle with chopped coriander.

this recipe comes from the Dublin wagamama where it was introduced as a special. Such was the take-up it has kept reappearing as a special ever since. It is full-flavoured and gutsy, a winter warmer to cheer you up and one for those summer days that are not quite as sunny as you might have hoped for. The dish takes a little longer to cook than most but the time involves everything simmering away gently so you can put your feet up and relax.

spiced vegetable stir fry

with chilli, soy sauce, miso soup and lemongrass

Previous pages: Happy staff mean happy customers. People, young and old and from all walks of life, enjoy the constant buzz and energy of the restaurants.

3 tablespoons vegetable oil

1 garlic clove, peeled and sliced

1 red chilli, trimmed, deseeded and sliced

1 lemongrass stalk, outer leaves removed, and sliced

1 red onion, peeled and chopped into 1cm (½in) pieces

2 small leeks, cut on the diagonal into 2.5cm (1in) lengths

12 mangetout

10 baby sweetcorn, halved lengthways

handful of beansprouts

4 pak choi, roughly chopped

pinch of salt

½ teaspoon sugar

2 tablespoons light soy sauce

250g (9 oz) noodles

600ml (1 pint) *miso* soup (see page 46)

Heat a wok over a medium heat for 1–2 minutes or until completely hot and almost smoking and add the vegetable oil. Add the garlic, chilli and lemongrass and stir fry for 30 seconds. Add the onion and leeks and stir fry for 1 minute. Add the remaining vegetables and season with salt, sugar and soy sauce. Stir fry for a further 3 minutes until all the vegetables are tender.

Cook the noodles in a large pan of boiling water for 2–3 minutes or until just tender. Drain thoroughly. Heat the *miso* soup in another pan. Divide the vegetables and noodles between 2 bowls and ladle over the hot *miso* soup.

You don't need a wok in order to stir fry, but it certainly makes life a lot easier. They are not expensive pieces of kit, particularly if you source one from an ethnic store.

yasai cha han

stir fried vegetable rice with soy sauce, miso soup and pickles

150g (5oz) Thai fragrant rice

4 tablespoons vegetable oil

14 button mushrooms, quartered

14 x 2cm (¾in) cubes of firm tofu

handful of baby sweetcorn

handful of sugarsnap peas

4 spring onions, trimmed and cut into 4cm (1½in) slices

1 teaspoon salt

3 tablespoons light soy sauce

2 eggs, beaten

to serve

miso soup (see page 46)

25g (1oz) pickles (see page 15)

Cook the rice in a large pan of boiling water for 2–3 minutes or until tender. Drain, refresh under cold running water and set aside.

Heat a wok over a medium heat for 1–2 minutes or until completely hot and almost smoking and add the vegetable oil. Add the mushrooms and stir fry for 2 minutes. Add the tofu and continue stir frying for a further 3 minutes, or until lightly coloured. Add the sweetcorn, sugarsnap peas and spring onions and stir fry over a medium heat until all the ingredients are warmed through. Add the rice, season with salt and soy sauce and stir fry for a further 2 minutes.

Add the eggs and stir fry vigorously until they are just cooked. Divide the stir fry mixture between 2 bowls. Heat the *miso* soup and serve separately, with the pickles on the side.

yasai dotenabe

stir fried vegetables and tofu with ginger, sesame oil and miso

200g (7oz) *udon* noodles
4 tablespoons vegetable oil
200g (7oz) firm tofu, cut into 2.5cm (1in) cubes
2 garlic cloves, peeled and crushed
1 tablespoon peeled and grated fresh ginger root
14 chestnut mushrooms, thickly sliced
½ red pepper, trimmed, deseeded and cut into strips
1 pak choi, trimmed, washed and quartered
1 small leek, trimmed and cut into strips
½ small carrot, peeled and cut into strips
1 teaspoon salt
1 teaspoon sugar
2 teaspoons light soy sauce
2 tablespoons sesame oil
600ml (1 pint) *miso* soup (see page 46)
few sprigs of coriander
12 pieces *menma* (canned bamboo shoots), drained

Cook the noodles in a large pan of boiling water for 2–3 minutes or until just tender. Drain and refresh under cold running water.

Heat a wok over a medium heat for 1–2 minutes or until completely hot and almost smoking and add the vegetable oil. Add the tofu and stir fry for 4–5 minutes until golden. Add the garlic and ginger and stir fry without colouring for 10 seconds. Add the mushrooms, red pepper, pak choi, leek and carrot and stir fry for 3 minutes until tender. Season with the salt, sugar, soy sauce and sesame oil and toss well.

Heat the *miso* soup. Divide the noodles and stir fry between 2 bowls and ladle over the hot soup. Top with the coriander and *menma*.

yasai yaki soba

stir fried vegetables with eggs, soba noodles and sesame seeds

250g (9oz) *soba* noodles

2 eggs

½ green pepper, trimmed, deseeded and cut into strips

½ red pepper, trimmed, deseeded and cut into strips

1 onion, peeled and thinly sliced

8 spring onions, trimmed and sliced

50g (2oz) button mushrooms, sliced

2 garlic cloves, peeled and finely chopped

handful of beansprouts

2 tablespoons *yaki soba* sauce (see page 32)

3 tablespoons vegetable oil

2 teaspoons pickled ginger (*gari*, see page 14)

1 tablespoon dried shallots

½ teaspoon sesame seeds

2 tablespoons *yasai soba* dressing (see page 39)

Cook the noodles in a large pan of boiling water for 2–3 minutes or until tender. Drain and refresh under cold running water. Beat the eggs in a bowl and add all the vegetables and the *yaki soba* sauce.

Heat a wok over a medium heat for 1–2 minutes or until completely hot and almost smoking and add the vegetable oil. Add the egg mixture and the cooked noodles and stir fry for 3 minutes. Divide between 2 bowls and top with the pickled ginger, shallots, sesame seeds and dressing.

noodles are cooked in exactly the same way as pasta; lots of boiling water. But because the noodles are already salted there is no need to salt the water, just make sure it is properly boiling.

yasai itameru

stir fried tofu with mixed vegetables, rice noodles and coconut ginger sauce

150g (5oz) rice noodles

3 tablespoons vegetable oil

1 tablespoon garlic paste (homemade or bought)

1 red chilli, trimmed, deseeded and finely chopped

200g (7oz) firm tofu, cut into 10 x 2.5cm (1in) cubes

3 pak choi, halved lengthways

1 red onion, peeled and thickly sliced

5 spring onions, trimmed and cut into 2.5cm (1in) lengths

1 small sweet potato, peeled and julienned

2 handfuls of beansprouts

1 teaspoon salt

1 teaspoon sugar

2 tablespoons light soy sauce

1 teaspoon sesame oil

250ml (9fl oz) coconut ginger sauce (see page 25)

12 coriander sprigs

1 lime, cut into slices

Cook the noodles in a large pan of boiling water for 2–3 minutes or until tender. Drain and refresh under cold running water.

Heat a wok over a medium heat for 1–2 minutes or until completely hot and almost smoking and add the vegetable oil. Stir in the garlic paste and red chilli, cook for 10 seconds, then add the tofu, pak choi, red onion, spring onions, sweet potato and beansprouts and stir fry for about 5 minutes.

Add the salt, sugar and soy sauce and stir fry for 4–5 minutes until tender. Remove from the heat, drizzle over the sesame oil and stir to combine.

In a separate pan, mix the coconut ginger sauce into the noodles and warm through over a low heat. Divide between 2 plates and top with the stir fry, coriander and lime slices.

For years, people in the West have tended to view tofu as a sort of non-food. Although it lacks flavour on its own, it is full of protein and is a great team player, liking nothing more than lots of gutsy flavours to soak up.

8
salads

What makes a good salad? For many it is the dressing and for years we have resisted repeated requests to reveal our recipe. No longer: it is given on page 32.

There is, however, rather more to a good salad than the dressing. A salad must provide variety, but it must also have direction, a focus, that ensures it does not become simply a basket for everything.

Popular consensus seems to demand leaves of some description. Loosely this means lettuce, but rather more unusual leaves – like rocket and misuna – also come into this category. Varying the leaves is one way to change a salad and allow it to evolve – more watercress and lamb's lettuce in winter perhaps; maybe greater use of Little Gem in summer.

Some of our salads use noodles and this picks up on the popular Japanese custom of eating cold *soba* noodles with a soy dipping sauce: comforting food to be enjoyed for its simplicity.

Defining what makes a salad a salad and a dish a dish is no easy task, particularly when you include warm salads. Most are eaten cold, however, and the idea is that all the ingredients are dressed. In Japanese cuisine dressed salads are called *aemono* and they make up one of the cooking styles used in a meal – the others being deep-fried (*agemono*), grilled (*yakimono*), sautéed (*itammono*), simmered (*nimono*), steamed (*mushimono*) and vinegared (*sunomono*).

How these different techniques are used enables the all-important balance to come into play. Not too much of any one thing, which even in a feast is important. Salads aim to refresh, to provide relief from the more complex and heavier dishes. Yet modern habits have meant they are now almost a meal in themselves.

In the summer months particularly, customers often have a salad and nothing else; a light and refreshing break from a hectic schedule. There is something very welcoming about a plate of colourful leaves with lots of other elements dotted about. Freshness is everything in a salad; crisp leaves, crunchy beansprouts and freshly cooked noodles all dressed with the heady delights of ginger, soy and sesame, coriander, *miso* and lime juice.

asparagus and green-tea noodle salad

with red pepper, chilli and coriander

6–9cm (2½–3½in) piece of *daikon* (mooli), peeled

1 small carrot, peeled

50g (2oz) *soba* noodles, cooked for 2–3 minutes in 200ml (7fl oz)
    boiling green tea and refreshed under cold running water

75g (3oz) buckwheat noodles, cooked for 2–3 minutes in
    boiling water and refreshed under cold running water

½ red pepper, trimmed, deseeded and cut into strips

1 red chilli, trimmed and sliced

20g (¾oz) *konbu* (see page 14), soaked in cold water, squeezed dry
    and cut into thin strips

2–3 tablespoons wagamama salad dressing (see page 32)

salt

1 small bunch of asparagus, spears halved lengthways

2 handfuls of beansprouts

1 tablespoon vegetable oil

handful of roughly chopped choi sum (see page 14)

small bunch of coriander, roughly chopped

Shred the *daikon* and carrot. (This is best done with a mouli-légumes or in a food processor to give you fine strands.) Place the *daikon* and carrot in a bowl of water with several ice cubes and place in the fridge for 1 hour to crisp. Drain well, mix together with the noodles, red pepper, red chilli, *konbu* and salad dressing, and season with salt. Divide between 2 plates.

Heat a griddle until smoking and toss the asparagus and beansprouts in the oil and a seasoning of salt. Cook on the griddle for 2–3 minutes, turning occasionally, until lightly charred. Add the choi sum towards the end so that it just wilts. Allow to cool, add to the rest of the salad and top with the coriander.

grilled tofu steak salad

with noodles, spring onions and sake

250g (9oz) firm tofu, cut into 2 steaks about 2cm (¾in) thick,
   each steak cut into 6 squares
4 tablespoons sake
2 tablespoons light soy sauce
2 teaspoons sesame oil
1 garlic clove, peeled and crushed
1 teaspoon peeled and grated fresh ginger root
salt
4 spring onions, sliced at an angle
a little vegetable oil
2 handfuls of salad leaves
3 tablespoons wagamama salad dressing (see page 32)
¼ cucumber, seeds removed and finely shredded
large handful of beansprouts, blanched for 10 seconds and
   refreshed under cold water
½ lime, sliced

Chargrilling is not difficult, but it does require confidence. Move your ingredients too quickly and you will soon discover they have stuck to the surface. Leave them alone for long enough and they have a way of unsticking, as if by magic.

Place the tofu on a clean tea towel, cover with another clean tea towel and place 2 chopping boards on top to press lightly. Leave for at least 30 minutes.

Combine the sake, soy sauce, sesame oil, garlic, ginger and salt to taste in a bowl, then add the tofu. Scatter over the spring onions and marinate for 45 minutes, tossing occasionally. Remove the tofu from the marinade, shaking off the spring onions and reserving the excess marinade.

Heat a griddle until smoking and lightly oil it with some kitchen paper dipped in vegetable oil. Place the tofu on the griddle and cook for 2–3 minutes on each side until golden brown. Toss the salad leaves in the salad dressing and place on the side of 2 plates.

Mix together the cucumber and blanched beansprouts and place alongside the salad leaves, topped with the lime slices. Arrange the tofu steaks around the salad and spoon over the reserved marinade.

rice noodle salad

with sweet potato, butternut squash, red pepper and sweet miso

1 small sweet potato, peeled and cut into 2cm (¾in) chunks

1 red pepper, trimmed, deseeded and thinly sliced

½ small butternut squash, peeled, deseeded and cut into 2cm (¾in) chunks

2 tablespoons vegetable oil

salt

175g (6oz) rice noodles, soaked in boiling water for 5 minutes or until tender

1 tablespoon chilli and coriander dressing (see page 22)

handful of mangetout, sliced on the diagonal

4 shiitake mushrooms, sliced

generous handful of beansprouts

3 tablespoons sweet *miso* dressing (see page 35)

2 sprigs of coriander

Preheat the oven to 200°C/400°F/Gas 6. Put the sweet potato, red pepper and butternut squash in a roasting pan, toss with the oil and season with salt. Roast for 20 minutes or until tender and then allow to cool.

Put all the ingredients except the coriander in a large bowl and toss. Pile into 2 bowls and top with the coriander.

smoked salmon salad

with egg noodles, spring onions and apricots

300ml (½ pint) green tea

150g (5oz) dried egg noodles

2 slices (or 75g/3oz) smoked salmon, cut into 3mm (⅛in) strips

½ red pepper, deseeded and cut into batons

1 small red onion, peeled and thinly sliced

6 spring onions, trimmed and sliced on the diagonal

1 red chilli, trimmed and thinly sliced

generous handful of beansprouts

50g (2oz) ready-to-eat dried apricots, thinly sliced

2 tablespoons light soy sauce

2 tablespoons vegetable oil

2 teaspoons chilli sauce (see page 27)

few sprigs of coriander

Strain the tea into a saucepan and bring to the boil. Add the noodles, turn off the heat and leave for 5 minutes or until tender. Drain well, refresh briefly under cold running water and set aside.

Combine the salmon, red pepper, red onion, spring onions, chilli, beansprouts and dried apricots in a large bowl. Stir through the soy sauce and oil and add the noodles. Divide between 2 plates and top with the chilli sauce and coriander.

Behind the casual, relaxed atmosphere of the restaurants there is a systemised approach aimed at ensuring customers experience the best service consistently. Feedback is encouraged and staff involvement is an integral part of the job. We believe in the whole idea of little improvements often. It allows us to evolve and develop.

salmon salad

chargrilled salmon with courgettes, peppers, cherry tomatoes and cucumber

Seared salmon is a winner every time; crisp, salty skin and underneath rich, full-flavoured flesh. Cooking is easy too, as the fish turns opaque before your very eyes.

2 courgettes, sliced
a little vegetable oil
salt
2 x 175g (6oz) salmon fillets
6 cherry tomatoes
½ cucumber, cut into strips
1 small carrot, peeled and cut into strips
½ red pepper, trimmed, deseeded and cut into strips
½ yellow pepper, trimmed, deseeded and cut into strips
6 tablespoons cucumber dressing (see page 26)
2 handfuls of mixed salad leaves
small handful of coriander leaves
1 lemon, cut into wedges

Heat a griddle until really hot. Lightly oil the courgette slices and spread them on the griddle in a single layer. Cook for 3 minutes on each side without disturbing. Transfer to a bowl and season with salt. Oil the salmon and cook for 4 minutes on each side, starting skin-side down, until opaque right through. Leave to cool.

Mix all the vegetables together with half the dressing and divide between 2 plates. Put the salad leaves on the side. Top with the salmon and coriander, and drizzle the rest of the dressing around the plate. Serve with a lemon wedge.

ginger chicken salad

with red pepper, spring onions and lime

Chicken breast is often used in restaurants even though it has a tendency to dryness. Thigh and leg meat, although darker, tends to be much more succulent and rich and often has more flavour. Both are interchangeable, but I know which one most chefs would favour.

vegetable oil, for deep frying
200g (7oz) boneless, skinless chicken thigh meat, cubed and marinated overnight in chilli and coriander dressing (see page 22)
4 tablespoons cornflour
2 handfuls of mixed salad leaves
4 tablespoons wagamama salad dressing (see page 32)
4 spring onions, trimmed and finely sliced on the diagonal
1 red pepper, deseeded and julienned
1 lime, halved

Pour enough oil into a heavy-bottomed pan to come two-thirds of the way up the sides. Place over a medium heat and heat until the oil reaches 180°C/350°F or until a cube of bread added to the oil browns in 30 seconds.

Remove the chicken from the marinade, shaking off any excess. Put the cornflour on a plate and dip the chicken in it to coat (or toss together in a polythene bag).

Lower the chicken into the pan and deep fry for 3–4 minutes or until golden and cooked through.

Divide the salad between 2 plates and place the chicken in the centre. Pour over the dressing. Top with the spring onions and red pepper and serve with a lime half.

Deep-frying is about the oil and the temperature. You need fresh, pure vegetable oil and the correct heat. Too cool and whatever you are cooking absorbs the oil. Too hot and the outside cooks before the inside has had a chance to blink.

tamarind chicken salad

with red onion, ginger and amai sauce

1 tablespoon vegetable oil

1 red onion, peeled and cut into chunks

2 boneless, skinless chicken breasts, cut into strips and marinated
   overnight in chilli and coriander dressing (see page 22)

generous handful of beansprouts

2 handfuls of mixed salad leaves

3 tablespoons wagamama salad dressing (see page 32)

2.5cm (1in) piece of fresh ginger root, peeled and grated

3 tablespoons *amai* sauce (see page 22)

½ cucumber, shredded

small handful of roughly chopped coriander

Heat a wok or large frying pan over a medium heat for 1–2 minutes or until completely hot and almost smoking and add the vegetable oil. Add the red onion and stir fry over a low-medium heat for 5 minutes until lightly caramelised.

Increase the heat and add the chicken, stir fry for 1 minute and then add the beansprouts. Stir fry for 2–3 minutes to finish cooking.

Toss the salad leaves in the dressing and divide between 2 plates. Place the chicken stir fry in the centre. Combine the grated ginger and *amai* sauce, spoon over and top with the shredded cucumber and coriander.

It may be the ramen dishes you are famous for, but for me it's the salads that really get me going!

Mark, Perth

warm stir fried chicken salad

marinated chicken with lime, chilli, coriander and toasted sesame seeds

4 boneless, skinless chicken thighs, cut into strips
3 tablespoons vegetable oil

for the marinade

1 teaspoon sesame oil
2 garlic cloves, peeled and crushed
2 teaspoons fish sauce (see page 14)
2 teaspoons light soy sauce
juice of 1 lime
2 teaspoons ground cumin
1 large red chilli, trimmed and chopped
2 teaspoons toasted sesame seeds (see below)

for the salad

2 handfuls of mixed salad leaves
2 tablespoons wagamama salad dressing (see page 32)
2 teaspoons toasted sesame seeds (see below)
1 tablespoon chopped coriander
1 lime, halved

Put all the ingredients for the marinade except the sesame seeds in a blender and blend until smooth, then stir in the sesame seeds. Put the chicken into a dish, pour over the marinade, cover with clingfilm and marinate for at least 2 hours (overnight if possible) in the fridge.

Heat a wok over a medium heat for 1–2 minutes or until completely hot and almost smoking and add the vegetable oil. Add the chicken, stirring constantly so the pieces cook evenly, and stir fry for 4–5 minutes until caramelised around the edges and cooked through.

Mix the salad leaves with the dressing. Divide between 2 plates and scatter over the toasted sesame seeds and chopped coriander. Top with the chicken and serve with a lime half on each plate.

to toast sesame seeds, heat a dry frying pan and when hot, add the seeds, tossing the pan so they are evenly coloured. Have a plate standing by to transport them on to or they are likely to burn.

spiced chicken salad

with star anise, sake, soy sauce and red pepper

200g (7oz) boneless, skinless chicken thigh meat,
    cut into 2.5cm (1in) cubes
2.5cm (1in) piece of fresh ginger root, peeled and finely grated
1 lemongrass stalk, outer leaves removed, finely sliced
2 garlic cloves, peeled, chopped and mashed with a little salt
1 red chilli, trimmed, deseeded and finely chopped
2 star anise
2 tablespoons sake
2 tablespoons light soy sauce
25g (1oz) cornflour
vegetable oil, for frying

for the salad

2 large handfuls of mixed salad leaves
4 spring onions, trimmed and finely sliced
1 red pepper, trimmed, deseeded and thinly sliced
2 tablespoons wagamama salad dressing (see page 32)
juice and zest of 1 lime

Put the chicken in a dish and scatter over the ginger, lemongrass, garlic, chilli, star anise, sake and soy sauce. Using your hands, turn everything gently for a few minutes. Cover with clingfilm and marinate for at least 1 hour, and overnight if possible, in the fridge.

Remove the chicken from the marinade, shaking off any excess. Put the cornflour in a bowl and dip the chicken in to coat. Heat a large frying pan with 2cm (¾in) of oil. Add the chicken and shallow fry for 8 minutes, turning occasionally.

Divide the salad leaves between 2 plates and top with the chicken. Scatter around the spring onions and red pepper. Combine the salad dressing with the juice and zest of the lime and drizzle over the top.

we marinate a lot of meat in the restaurants. This is done by combining the meat and the marinade in a plastic bag and gently massaging it. The same principal works well at home, too. Simply dropping the meat into the marinade is not enough; you have to work the two together to get an exchange of flavours.

beef itameru

marinated beef stir fry with red onion, dressed leaves and amai sauce

300g (10½oz) sirloin steak, trimmed and cut into thin strips

2 tablespoons chilli and coriander dressing (see page 22)

3 tablespoons vegetable oil

1 small red onion, peeled and cut into chunks

2 handfuls of beansprouts

2 large handfuls of mixed peppery salad leaves

2 tablespoons wagamama salad dressing (see page 32)

2 teaspoons peeled and grated fresh ginger root

3 tablespoons *amai* sauce (see page 22)

¼ cucumber, deseeded and cut into thin strips

small bunch of coriander, roughly chopped

Combine the beef and chilli and coriander dressing and toss so the meat is well coated. Cover with clingfilm and marinate for at least 1 hour, and overnight if possible, in the fridge.

Heat a wok or large, heavy-bottomed frying pan over a medium heat for 1–2 minutes or until completely hot and almost smoking and add the vegetable oil. Add the onion and stir fry for 2 minutes until soft. Increase the heat to high and cook for a further 2 minutes until lightly caramelised. Add the beef and stir fry for 1–2 minutes or until lightly golden. Tip in the beansprouts and cook for 2–3 minutes, then remove from the heat.

Place the salad leaves in a large bowl and drizzle over the salad dressing. Toss until all the leaves are coated and divide between 2 plates. Combine the ginger and *amai* sauce. Pile the beef up in the centre of the plates and pour over the sauce. Top with the cucumber and coriander.

All our kitchens are open plan. The transparency means the chefs get to see how and what customers are eating and customers have full view of all the activity in the kitchen. This is a key part of the wagamama concept and it allows food to be prepared and delivered quickly.

hot beef salad

with chilli, crab salad and soy sauce

3 tablespoons vegetable oil

1 red onion, peeled and cut into half-moon slices

110g (4oz) broccoli florets or courgettes, cut into bite-sized pieces

250g (9oz) sirloin or rump steak, cut into thin strips

handful of mangetout, thinly sliced lengthways

2 garlic cloves, peeled and crushed

1 red chilli, trimmed, deseeded and sliced

1 crabstick, shredded (optional)

150g (5oz) beansprouts

1 teaspoon sugar

1 teaspoon salt

1 tablespoon light soy sauce

1 lime, halved

2 tablespoons fried shallots (available from Oriental stores)

4 sprigs of coriander

Heat a wok over a medium heat for 1–2 minutes or until completely hot and almost smoking and add the vegetable oil. Add the red onion and broccoli and stir fry for 2–3 minutes until lightly browned. Add the beef and stir fry for about 5 minutes until lightly browned. Add the mangetout, garlic, chilli, crabstick and beansprouts and stir fry for a further 2–3 minutes. Add the sugar, salt and soy sauce and toss quickly. Divide between 2 plates, squeeze over the juice from the lime and sprinkle with the shallots and coriander.

Your salads have made me completely re-invent what I eat during the summer months. All that colour and crunch leaves me feeling totally satisfied. I can hardly bear to look at a sandwich these days!

Helena, Western Australia

9
desserts

Most of these desserts are based on fruit, a reflection in part of the Japanese tendency to end a meal with fruit. There are many reasons for this, not least the long-standing aversion to dairy products and the fact that most Japanese homes do not have an oven, so baking is not a traditional activity.

We also concentrate on fruit as it is a healthy and light option to end a meal. The sense of well-being is central to the whole philosophy of wagamama: eat well and live well. So we chargrill fruit, infuse coconut into the odd creamy concoction – no need to be healthy all the time! – and gently poach pears in sake with spices for extra interest.

We have deliberately kept this chapter short. While confectionary in Japan is a very big – and sweet – part of the national cuisine, the more normal route to finish a meal is with carefully cut fruit, maybe with the benefit of a spice or two for added zest. This is what we do with papaya, for example, but the recipe will work equally well with mango, peaches and nectarines when they are in season.

As with vegetables, the cutting, in terms of size as well as shape, is a very important part of the preparation. A bowl of fruit placed in the middle of the table for dessert is not as easy to break into as a plate of fruit which has been cut and fashioned enticingly. This is not to say a display has to be intricate or formal, but a variety of shapes lends interest and if you and your guests are eating with chopsticks it allows you to have one large plate and people can then pick as they like.

For those of you who desire something more substantial, we have added in some cooked desserts: fruit *katsu* is one, which is a variety of fruit dipped in breadcrumbs and then briefly deep fried. The green tea drizzle cake is another. Our customers get through an awful lot of green tea and one of our chefs came up with the idea of using this rather unique flavour in a cake. It tastes delicious served with a dollop of crème fraîche.

The perfect partner for these desserts is, of course, ice cream, hardly traditional but tasty nonetheless. Which only goes to reinforce the idea that while wagamama has its origins in Japan, it is quite unique, a combination of numerous different influences and aspects, something which is altogether rather more a sum than a collection of parts. Ice cream, anyone?

lemongrass and chilli crème caramel

with sake and star anise

200ml (7fl oz) milk

2 lemongrass stalks, outer leaves removed, slightly bashed

1 dried red chilli

2 tablespoons sake

1 cinnamon stick

1 star anise

50g (2oz) white sugar

1 egg and 2 yolks

2 x 150ml (¼ pint) ramekin dishes

for the caramel

4 tablespoons water

50g (2oz) white sugar

Put the milk, lemongrass, chilli, sake, cinnamon stick and star anise in a pan and place over a low heat for 15 minutes, without letting it come to the boil. Turn off the heat and leave to infuse.

Preheat the oven to 150°C/300°F/Gas 2. First prepare the caramel. Put the water and the sugar in a small pan over a very low heat, without boiling, until dissolved. Turn up the heat and boil until golden. Carefully pour into the bottom of the ramekins.

Whisk the sugar, egg and yolks in a mixing bowl until light. Strain the infused milk on to the eggs, mix well and pour over the caramel. Place the ramekins in a roasting tray on the middle shelf of the oven and fill the tray with enough boiling water to reach halfway up the sides of the ramekins. Bake for 40–45 minutes until set, with a slight wobble, but not coloured. Allow to cool completely in the roasting tray. Turn out on to 2 plates and serve.

introducing rice to a crème brulée (right) may seem like sacrilege to some yet the inherent creaminess of the rice works wonders both for flavour and texture. You can play around with other rices too, Italian arborio produces a richer, more rounded result and basmati has its fans.

coconut rice brulée

with cinnamon

2 tablespoons Japanese rice
200ml (7fl oz) coconut milk
100ml (3½fl oz) water
1 cinnamon stick
3 egg yolks
50g (2oz) white sugar
50ml (2fl oz) double cream
1½ tablespoons demerara sugar, for glazing
2 x 150ml (¼ pint) ramekin dishes

Preheat the oven to 150°C/300°F/Gas 2. Put the rice, half the coconut milk, the water and cinnamon in a pan and bring to the boil. Simmer gently for 15 minutes, covered, stirring occasionally to prevent sticking. Turn off the heat and leave to stand, covered, for a further 10 minutes until the rice is tender and the liquid has been absorbed. Divide between the 2 ramekins. Whisk the egg yolks with the white sugar until light.

Heat the cream and the remaining coconut milk in a small pan and whisk into the egg and sugar mixture. Stir to combine, then pour over the rice. Place the ramekins in a roasting tray on the middle shelf of the oven and fill the tray with enough boiling water to reach halfway up the sides of the ramekins. Bake for 45 minutes until almost set (there should be a slight wobble). Remove from the oven and allow to cool completely in the roasting tray. To serve, sprinkle the top with demerera sugar and *brulée*, either using a blow torch or under a very hot grill, until golden and crispy.

The essence of a good brulée lies in the just-set custard and a thin crust that yields to a little pressure. The ideal route, although risky, is to up-end the ramekin once you have dusted the sugar so only a fine coating is left. Trouble is, this can lead to custard on the floor!

fresh papaya

with chilli, ginger and lime

225g (8oz) papaya peeled, deseeded and cut widthways into 5mm
 (¼in) slices
2.5cm (1in) piece of fresh ginger root, peeled and cut into thin strips
½ red chilli, trimmed, deseeded and finely chopped
1 lime, quartered, to serve

Arrange the papaya on 2 plates. Scatter over the ginger strips and the chopped
chilli. Serve with the lime wedges to squeeze over.

fruit katsu

golden fruit with ice cream and mint

1 tablespoon *shichimi* flour (see page 19)

1 egg, beaten

335g (12oz) coconut *panko* breadcrumbs (see page 19)

2 x 5mm (¼in) slices of fresh pineapple, peeled and cored

1 banana, peeled and cut into 4cm (1½in) slices

1 apple, peeled, cored and cut into wedges

vegetable oil, for deep frying

to serve

vanilla ice cream

sprigs of mint

Place the *shichimi* flour in a bowl, the beaten egg in another and the breadcrumbs in a third. Dip the fruit first in the flour, then the egg and finally the breadcrumbs.

Fill a pan one-third full of oil and heat to 180°C/350°F or until a cube of bread added to the oil browns in 30 seconds. Deep fry the fruit in batches until golden brown. Remove from the oil and drain well on kitchen paper.

To serve, divide the fruit between 2 bowls and top with a scoop of ice cream and a sprig of fresh mint.

There aren't many restaurants where kids are encouraged to draw all over the placemats! My own two grab the crayons, order cha han or yaki soba and a drink and settle in. They both seem to pick up on the buzz and the friendliness of the staff. It's become part of their lives and will continue to be for some time probably.

banana katsu

with ice cream, redcurrants and mint

1 tablespoon flour
1 egg, beaten
3 tablespoons *panko* breadcrumbs
2 large bananas, peeled but left whole
vegetable oil, for deep frying
icing sugar, for dusting
4 scoops of vanilla ice cream, to serve

to decorate
few sprigs of redcurrants
sprigs of mint

Place the flour in a bowl, the beaten egg in another and the breadcrumbs in a third. Dip the bananas first in the flour, then in the egg and finally in the breadcrumbs until coated. Put 5cm (2in) of the vegetable oil in a pan and heat to 180°C (350°F), or until a cube of bread added to the oil browns in 30 seconds.

Deep fry the bananas for 3–4 minutes or until golden brown. Remove carefully with a slotted spoon, drain on kitchen paper and dust with icing sugar.

Divide between 2 plates and serve with the ice cream. Decorate with some redcurrants and mint.

The breadcrumbs are key here – Japanese really are the best – but so too is the oil and its tempera-ture. Use a pure vegetable oil every time and ensure it is hot enough or you'll end up absorbing too much of the oil into the breadcrumbs.

chargrilled pineapple

and coconut broth

400ml (14fl oz) canned coconut milk
75g (3oz) white sugar
juice of 1 lime and zest of ½
5cm (2in) piece of lemongrass stalk, outer leaves removed, sliced
4 x 1cm (½in) slices of fresh pineapple, peeled and cored
  (or use canned pineapple rings)

Put the coconut milk, 50g (2oz) of the sugar, the lime juice and zest and lemongrass in a heavy-bottomed pan over a medium heat and simmer gently for 5 minutes. Remove and set aside to infuse and cool.

   Heat a griddle pan over a high heat until almost smoking. Sprinkle the remaining sugar over the pineapple slices. When the pan is hot, cook the pineapple for 1 minute on each side. Strain the broth, reheat gently, pour into 2 bowls and add the pineapple rings.

marinated mango

with coconut sorbet

110g (4oz) white sugar
125ml (4fl oz) water
25g (1oz) fresh ginger root, peeled and grated
1 star anise
juice and zest of 1 lime
1 ripe mango, peeled, stoned and cut into 5mm (¼in) slices
2 scoops of coconut or lime sorbet, to serve

Put the sugar, water, ginger, star anise, lime juice and zest in a pan over a medium heat until the sugar is dissolved. Increase the heat and simmer for 15 minutes until fragrant and syrupy, but still clear. Set aside to cool.

   When cool, add the sliced mango and leave to marinate overnight in the fridge. Fan the slices of mango in a circle in the centre of a serving plate, spoon over some of the syrup and serve with a scoop of sorbet.

spiced fruit compote

with sake

200ml (7fl oz) water
110g (4oz) white sugar
2 star anise
1 cinnamon stick
1 dried red chilli
2 oranges (you need the zest of 1 and the juice of 2)
1 apple, peeled, cored and cut into 1cm (½in) cubes
1 Chinese pear, peeled, cored and cut into 1cm (½in) cubes
12 dried apricots
50g (2oz) dried banana
50g (2oz) dried papaya
50g (2oz) dried mango
12 lychees, peeled, stoned and halved
75ml (3fl oz) sake

Put the water, sugar, star anise, cinnamon, chilli, orange juice and zest in a pan. Bring to the boil, cook for 5 minutes and then lower the heat to a simmer. Add the apple, pear and all the dried fruit, cover and simmer for 45 minutes–1 hour or until tender.

   Transfer to a bowl and add the lychees. Heat the sake and, just as it comes to the boil, pour over the fruits, stir and serve.

sake is a complicated subject and, like wine, they vary in quality. Most are delicious, however, and you need to experiment to find those that you prefer. Sake is served both warm and cold, the latter being the preferred route for most westerners when it is often compared to a dry fino sherry.

fruit yakitori

with lime syrup

100ml (3½fl oz) water

110g (4oz) white sugar

juice and zest of 2 limes

½ pineapple, cut into 2.5cm (1in) chunks
   (or use canned pineapple chunks)

2 bananas, cut into 4cm (1½in) pieces

3 kiwi fruit, peeled and quartered

4 bamboo skewers, soaked in cold water for 2 hours

Put the water, half the sugar, the lime juice and zest in a small pan. Bring to the boil, lower the heat and simmer gently for 10–15 minutes or until thick and syrupy.

Thread the fruit on to the skewers. Scatter over the remaining sugar evenly. Heat a griddle or grill and cook until the fruit is golden and slightly charred, turning occasionally. Drizzle with the lime syrup.

sake poached pears

with warm chocolate sauce

600ml (1 pint) water
8 tablespoons sake
225g (8oz) white sugar
2 star anise
1 cinnamon stick
juice and zest of 1 lime
2 ripe but firm Chinese pears, peeled
    but left whole
for the chocolate sauce
150ml (¼ pint) double cream
50g (2oz) butter
75g (3oz) dark chocolate
white sugar, to taste
zest of 1 lime

Put the water, sake, sugar, star anise, cinnamon, lime juice and zest in a small, deep pan and bring to the boil. Simmer vigorously for 5 minutes, then lower the heat to a gentle simmer. Add the pears, cover and simmer for about 45 minutes, or until tender. Remove from the heat and leave to cool in the liquor.

To make the sauce, place all the ingredients except the lime zest in a small pan and heat gently until melted and smooth. Stir in the lime zest.

To serve, place the cooked pears on a chopping board, cut each one in half and remove the core. Place in 2 serving bowls and pour over the chocolate sauce.

The poaching needs to be gentle, the objective being not just to soften the pears, but to infuse them with the spicy delights of star anise and cinnamon. Other spices that work well are cloves and cardamoms but don't be tempted to go overboard, or you'll end up with something rather confused.

the chocolate needs to be of good quality; dark and forbidding but full of complex flavours. There is something about spicy food that makes chocolate seem a popular way to finish.

green tea drizzle cake

with crème fraîche

serves 6–8

110g (4oz) plain flour

10g (½oz) green tea powder (optional)

½ teaspoon baking powder

110g (4oz) caster sugar

4 eggs

75g (3oz) butter, melted and cooled

crème fraîche, to serve

for the green tea syrup

2 tablespoons green tea leaves

150ml (¼ pint) boiling water

150g (5oz) caster sugar

Preheat the oven to 180°C/350°F/Gas 4. Grease a 20cm (8in) round cake tin and base-line with greaseproof paper.

Sift the flour, green tea powder (if using) and baking powder into a large bowl. Put the sugar and eggs into a large heatproof bowl over a pan of barely simmering water. Using an electric whisk, beat the sugar and eggs for 2–3 minutes until the mixture trebles in volume, lightens in colour and is the consistency of lightly whipped cream.

Sift in the flour mixture and drizzle the melted butter down the side of the bowl, then gently fold in until incorporated. The mixture should not be beaten or over-worked. Pour into the prepared tin. Bake on the bottom shelf of the oven for 30–35 minutes, or until the cake is golden and firm to the touch and coming away from the side of the tin. A skewer inserted into the centre should come out clean.

While the cake is cooking, make the green tea syrup. Stir the green tea leaves into the boiling water and leave to stand for 2–3 minutes to create a strong infusion. Strain the tea into a small pan with the sugar and set over a very low heat until the sugar has completely dissolved. Increase the heat and boil rapidly for 5 minutes until you have a light syrup. Remove 3–4 tablespoons of the syrup and set aside to cool. Keep the rest of the syrup warm while the cake is cooking.

As soon as the cake is cooked, remove from the oven but leave in the tin for a few minutes to cool slightly. Skewer the cake surface and drizzle the warm syrup slowly and evenly over the top of the cake. Leave to cool completely in the tin. Mix the cooled reserved syrup with the crème fraîche, then cover and chill.

Remove the cake from the tin and peel away the greaseproof paper. Serve with a dollop of green-tea-spiked crème fraîche.

10
juices
and drinks

Drinks on the wagamama menu are diverse and varied. We serve lots of raw juices – both fruit and vegetable – as well as beer, wine, soft drinks and, of course, tea. The tea is green, the colour a result of the leaves being steamed before they are dried, which prevents them turning black.

We make a lot of our juices, as much for their flavour as for their healthy attributes. All are refreshing, some (like the carrot juice) are spiced with a little ginger, while others are left plain and natural, like the fruit juice blend of apple, orange and passionfruit.

To make these juices, you do require a dedicated juicer. These vary quite a lot in price and it may be worth considering a cheaper model while you experiment to see how frequently you come to use one. The quantities here are for one large or two small glasses.

Many diners in the restaurants start with a fresh juice and then move on to tea, but a great number also have a soft drink or beer.

Most of our beers are from the East. They tend to have an alcohol rating around the 5 per cent mark, which ensures a strength of character sufficient to cope with the food. Lower-rated lagers can be drowned out by the big flavours and this is also true of softer beers, like pale ales.

Wines are chosen to complement the food, so the whites tend to be dry and crisp or quite full-flavoured and fragrant to stand up to the spicing. On the red front, light and fruity works best – anything too tannic tends to clash with the spices. Sake is also popular and highlights the need for a wine with quite a big flavour, so leave the delicate bottles for another time.

Green tea is probably the most traditional of all the drinks we serve. This is a large subject and not something that can be covered in sufficient detail here. Suffice to say that there are a number of different grades of green tea and a great deal of ceremony associated with drinking it.

What is best to drink with the dishes in this book is purely a matter of preference. And while the idea of not drinking when eating can seem odd, given the amount written about pairing food with suitable beverages, it is a route well worth trying. Consider a bowl of wagamama *ramen* by itself and then sit and relax over a cup of green tea. The world can seem a better place.

pineapple and watermelon juice

175g (6oz) pineapple, peeled, cored and cut into cubes
175g (6oz) watermelon flesh
small handful of coriander, including stalks
½ red chilli, trimmed and halved
50ml (2fl oz) orange juice

Push all the ingredients through a juicer and pour into 2 glasses.

raw juice

We wondered how the raw juice would be received when we first put it on the menu.
Its name seems almost too healthy, but it has walked out the door from the first day
it went on sale.

1 apple, peeled, cored and halved
200ml (7fl oz) orange juice
1 tomato, cored
5cm (2in) piece of cucumber, roughly chopped
4 medium carrots, peeled and finely chopped

Push all the ingredients through a juicer and pour into 2 glasses.

*Above left: pineapple and
watermelon juice.
Above right: raw juice.*

apple and cranberry juice .

A good juicer tends to generate a rather attractive froth, which sits on the top of the juice much like milk on a cappuccino. The staff have competitions to see how perfect they can make the froth.

6 apples, peeled, cored and halved
75g (3oz) cranberries

Push the apples and cranberries through a juicer and pour into 2 glasses.

carrot juice

5cm (2in) piece of fresh ginger root, peeled and roughly chopped
6 medium carrots, peeled and finely sliced

Push the ingredients through a juicer and pour into 2 glasses.

Below left: apple and cranberry juice.
Below right: carrot juice.

apple and orange juice

4 apples, peeled, cored and halved
200ml (7fl oz) orange juice

Push the apples through a juicer, combine with the orange juice and pour into 2 glasses.

apple, carrot and watercress juice

4 apples, peeled, cored and halved
2 handfuls of watercress, washed
4 medium carrots, peeled and finely chopped

Push the apples, then the watercress and finally the carrots through a juicer and pour into 2 glasses.

apple, passionfruit and orange juice

1 passionfruit
4 apples, peeled, cored and halved
200ml (7fl oz) orange juice

Halve the passionfruit, scoop out the seeds and pulp and push with the apples through a juicer. Combine with the orange juice and pour into 2 glasses.

apple, carrot and celery juice

4 medium carrots, peeled and finely chopped
2 celery sticks, finely sliced
3 apples, peeled, cored and halved

Push all the ingredients through a juicer and pour into 2 glasses.

apple, celery and mint juice

6 apples, peeled, cored and halved
2 sprigs of mint (including stalks), roughly chopped
2 celery sticks, finely sliced

Push all the ingredients through a juicer and pour into 2 glasses.

Sales of juices have rocketed in recent years. It used to be tea, beer, fizzy drinks and then wine, but now juices top the list. Customers say they like the flavour and the healthy aspect and undoubtedly you tend to feel rather pleased with yourself after sinking something packed so full of goodness.

index

a

Amai sauce, 22
Amai udon, 86
Apples
  apple and cranberry juice, 187
  apple and orange juice, 188
  apple, carrot and celery juice, 189
  apple, carrot and watercress juice, 188
  apple, celery and mint juice, 189
  raw juice, 186
Asparagus and green-tea noodle salad,
  154

b

Banana *katsu*, 176
Barbecue sauce, 29
Beef
  beef *itameru*, 167
  chilli beef *ramen*, 121
  hot beef salad, 169
  pork and beef cabbage rolls, 122
  seared beef *sashimi*, 61
  zasai beef *gohan*, 133
Breadcrumbs, 15
  coconut *panko* breadcrumbs, 19

c

Cabbage
  pickled, 15
  pork and beef cabbage rolls, 122
Caramelised sweet potatoes, 43
Carrots
  apple, carrot and celery juice, 189
  apple, carrot and watercress juice, 188
  carrot juice, 187
Celery
  apple, carrot and celery juice, 189
  apple, celery and mint juice, 189
Cha han, 67
Char sui sauce, 14
Chicken, 62
  cha han, 67
  chicken and prawn hot pot, 70
  chicken chilli *men*, 65
  chicken *gyoza*, 56
  chicken *ramen*, 68
  chicken rice noodles, 78
  chicken stocks, 17, 18
  chicken *tama* rice, 64
  ginger chicken salad, 162
  ginger chicken *teppan*, 69
  marinated chicken stir fry, 79
  marinating, 62
  miso ramen, 77
  negima yakitori, 42
  spiced chicken salad, 166
  tamarind chicken salad, 163
  teriyaki chicken stir fry, 72
  thigh meat, using, 41
  tori kara age, 58
  warm stir fried chicken salad, 164
  yaki soba, 110
  yaki udon, 73
  zasai chicken *gohan*, 81

Chikuwa, 14
Chilli
  chilli and coriander dressing, 22
  chilli beef *ramen*, 121
  chilli *ramen* sauce, 23
  chilli sauce, 27
  ebi chilli men, 87
  ginger chilli mushrooms, 139
  lemongrass and chilli crème caramel, 172
  sweet chilli dipping sauce, 15
  yasai chilli men, 137
  zasai chilli sauce, 36
Choi sum, 14
Coconut
  coconut ginger sauce, 25
  coconut *panko* breadcrumbs, 19
  coconut rice brulée, 173
Cod
  poached cod with shiitake, 92
  sweet *miso* cod, 93
Cooking styles, 11
Coriander
  chilli and coriander dressing, 22
Cranberries
  apple and cranberry juice, 187
Cucumber dressing, 26
Cured marinated salmon salad, 53
Curry oil, 19

d

Dashi, 14, 18, 46
  dashi no moto, 14
Desserts, 171
Dressings
  chilli and coriander dressing, 22
  cucumber dressing, 26
  garlic herb oil, 35
  sweet *miso* dressing, 35
  wagamama salad dressing, 32
  yasai soba dressing, 39
Drinks, 185
Duck
  shichimi spiced duck *ramen*, 118

e

Ebi chilli men, 87
Ebi gyoza, 51
Ebi katsu sauce, 27
Ebi katsu, 52
Ebi kuzu kiri sauce, 28
Ebi yakitori, 84
Edamame, 14, 46
Enoki, 14
Equipment, 9

f

Fish, 83
  dashi, 18
  kai sen udon, 95
  kamaboko-aka, 14
  katsuo bushi, 14
  seafood *ramen*, 114
  spicy fish powder, 15
Fish sauce, 14
Fruit
  fruit *katsu*, 175
  fruit *yakitori*, 179
  raw juice, 186
  spiced fruit compote, 178

g

Gari, 14
Garlic herb oil, 35
Ginger
  coconut ginger sauce, 25
  gari, 14
  ginger chicken salad, 162
  ginger chilli mushrooms, 139
  mackerel with soy and ginger, 115
  soy, sake and ginger marinade, 33
Green tea, 185
  asparagus and green-tea noodle
    salad, 154
  green tea drizzle cake, 182
Grilled sea bream, 88
Grilled teriyaki sea bass, 88
Grilled tofu steak salad, 157
Gyoza skins, 14
Gyoza sauce, 33
Gyozas, 41

h, i, j

Haddock
  smoked haddock *ramen*, 96
Hake *tempura*, 102
Home-cured spiced swordfish steak, 90
Hot beef salad, 169
Ingredients, 14, 15
Juices, 185

k, l

Kai sen udon, 95
Kamaboko-aka, 14
Kare lomen sauce, 38
Katsuo bushi, 14
Konbu, 14
Konnyaku, 14
Lamb *kare lomen*, 130
Lemongrass and chilli crème caramel, 172

m

Mackerel with soy and ginger, 115
Mango, marinated, 177
Marinated chicken stir fry, 79
Marinated vegetable *ramen*, 140
Meat, preparing, 16, 116
Melon
  pineapple and watermelon juice, 186
Menma, 14
Mikku powder, 14
Mirin, 14
Miso, 14
  miso paste, 14, 19
  miso ramen, 77
  miso soup and pickles, 46
  rice noodle soup, 137
  sweet *miso* cod, 93
  sweet *miso* dressing, 35
Monkfish *yakitori*, 113
Moyashi soba, 136
Mushrooms
  enoki, 14
  ginger chilli mushrooms, 139
  poached cod with shiitake, 92
  shiitake, 15
Mussels
  oven-steamed mussels, 55

n, o

Noodles
  cooking, 17
  liquid, ratio to, 17
  types of, 14, 15
Oranges
  apple and orange juice, 188
Oven-steamed mussels, 55
Oyster sauce, 15

p

Panko breadcrumbs, 15
  coconut *panko* breadcrumbs, 19
Papaya, fresh, 174
Pears
  sake poached pears, 181
Pineapple
  chargrilled pineapple, 177
  pineapple and watermelon juice, 186
Poached cod with shiitake, 92
Pork
  pork and beef cabbage rolls, 122
  pork belly hot pot, 123
  pork *char siu men*, 128
  roasted honey pork *ramen*, 125
  tonkatsu, 129
Prawns
  amai udon, 86
  chicken and prawn hot pot, 70
  ebi chilli men, 87
  ebi gyoza, 51
  ebi katsu, 52
  ebi yakitori, 84
  yaki soba, 110
Pumpkin curry, 143

r

Ramen dishes, 21
Raw salad, 47
Rice, 15
  chicken *tama* rice, 64
  cooking, 17
Rice noodles
  chicken rice noodles, 78
  rice noodle soup, 137
  rice noodle salad, 158
Roasted honey pork *ramen*, 125

s

Sake, 15
  soy, sake and ginger marinade, 33
Sake amiyaki gohan, 105
Salads, 153
  asparagus and green-tea noodle
    salad, 154
  beef *itameru*, 167
  cured marinated salmon salad, 53
  ginger chicken salad, 162
  grilled tofu steak salad, 157
  hot beef salad, 169
  raw salad, 47
  rice noodle salad, 158
  salmon salad, 161
  seared beef *sashimi*, 61
  smoked salmon salad, 159
  spiced chicken salad, 166
  tamarind chicken salad, 163

  warm stir fried chicken salad, 164
Salmon
  cured marinated salmon salad, 53
  sake amiyaki gohan, 105
  salmon hot pot, 108
  salmon *korroke*, 107
  salmon *ramen*, 104
  salmon salad, 161
  smoked salmon salad, 159
  spiced *sake soba*, 109
Sauces
  amai sauce, 22
  barbecue sauce, 29
  chilli *ramen* sauce, 23
  chilli sauce, 27
  coconut ginger sauce, 25
  ebi katsu sauce, 27
  ebi kuzu kiri sauce, 28
  gyoza sauce, 33
  kare lomen sauce, 38
  soy, sake and ginger marinade, 33
  teriyaki sauce, 28
  tori kara age sauce, 39
  tsuyu sauce, 36
  yaki soba dipping sauce, 32
  yakitori sauce, 37
  yasai vinegar, 37
  zasai chilli sauce, 36
Sea bass
  grilled teriyaki sea bass, 88
  suzuki amiyaki soba, 101
Sea bream, grilled, 88
Seafood
  kai sen udon, 95
  seafood *ramen*, 114
Seared beef *sashimi*, 61
Shaoshing wine, 15
Shichimi, 15
Shichimi spiced duck *ramen*, 118
Shichimi spiced flour, 19
Smoked haddock *ramen*, 96
Smoked salmon salad, 159
Soy, sake and ginger marinade, 33
Soy sauce, 15
Soya beans
  edamame, 14, 46
Spiced chicken salad, 166
Spiced fruit compote, 178
Spiced *sake soba*, 109
Spiced tofu *katsu*, 57
Spiced vegetable stir fry, 146
Stir frying, 10
Stocks, 16
  chicken, 17, 18
  dashi, 18
  vegetable, 18
Suzuki amiyaki soba, 101
Sweet *miso* cod, 93
Sweet *miso* dressing, 35
Sweet potatoes, caramelised, 43
Swordfish
  home-cured spiced swordfish steak, 90
Szechuan vegetables, 15

t

Tamarind chicken salad, 163
Teriyaki sauce, 15, 28

Tofu, 15, 135
  grilled tofu steak salad, 157
  spiced tofu *katsu*, 57
  yasai itameru, 151
Tonkatsu, 129
Tori kara age sauce, 39
Tori kara age, 58
Tsuyu sauce, 15, 36

v

Vegetables, 135
  ebi yakitori, 84
  marinated vegetable *ramen*, 140
  moyashi soba, 136
  pickled, 15
  preparing, 16
  raw salad, 47
  spiced vegetable stir fry, 146
  Szechuan, 15
  vegetable *dashi* broth, 18
  vegetable stock, 18
  wagamama ramen, 74
  yasai cha han, 147
  yasai chilli men, 137
  yasai dotenabe, 148
  yasai gyoza, 49
  yasai korroke, 142
  yasai yaki soba, 149
  yasai yakitori, 48
Vinegar
  amai sauce, 22
  chilli *ramen* sauce, 23
  yasai vinegar, 37

w

wagamama *ramen*, 74
wagamama salad dressing, 32
Wakame, 15
Warm stir fried chicken salad, 164
Watercress
  apple, carrot and watercress juice, 188
White pepper, 15
Wines, 185
Wok, 9
  seasoning, 11

y

Yaki soba, 110
Yaki soba dipping sauce, 32
Yaki udon, 73
Yakitori sauce, 37
Yasai cha han, 147
Yasai chilli men, 137
Yasai dotenabe, 148
Yasai gyoza, 49
Yasai itameru, 151
Yasai korroke, 142
Yasai soba dressing, 39
Yasai vinegar, 37
Yasai yaki soba, 149
Yasai yakitori, 48

z

Zasai beef gohan, 133
Zasai chicken *gohan*, 81
Zasai chilli sauce, 36

useful addresses

While not at all comprehensive, the following shops are good sources of Oriental ingredients and equipment:

Holland

Toko Dun Yong
Stormsteeg/Zeedijk 83
1012 BD Amsterdam
Netherlands

Yama Products
Rutherfordweg 2
3504 AC Utrecht
Netherlands

United Kingdom

Any of the supermarkets in Chinatown, London.

Wing Yip
395 Edgware Road
London NW2

(And various branches in Croydon, Manchester and Birmingham.)

Hanson Chinese Supermarket
2 Carrington Street
Nottingham

Lims Chinese Supermarket
63 Cambridge Street
Glasgow G3 6QX
Scotland

Ireland

Asia market
18 Drury Street
Dublin 2

Oriental Emporium
25 South Great Georges Street
Dublin 2

Australia

Japanese and Asian food is widely available in Australia from any of the supermarkets in Chinatown, Sydney and around the country.

author acknowledgements

Of the very many people who helped in the process of this book I would especially like to thank Paul O'Farrell, who initially commissioned the project and then had the vision to sit back and watch it happen; to Kyle Cathie, who has a canny sense of the creative; Ian Neill who loomed large at all the right moments and Jay Travis, who managed to enthuse and teach me about cricket at the same time.

A book like this is very much a team project and I would like to thank Sarah Epton, Vanessa Courtier, Joss Herd, Deirdre Rooney and Wei Tang, all of whom influenced the project hugely.

The staff at wagamama were all enormously helpful, particularly the head chefs worldwide – Australia, Holland, Ireland and the UK – who contributed recipes and suggestions with enthusiasm. To Adrian McCormack, Lisa King, Andreas Karlsson, Dinah Meister, Peter Hill, Sarah Crawford, Mark Tilson, Gary Virdee and Milroy Cruize for early insights which were crucial. The task of transferring recipes from restaurant kitchen to domestic setting was greatly assisted by Jason Pettit, whose unfailing good humour got us through most of the hurdles with a smile. To Vikki O'Neill, who has perfected the art of the possible like no one else.

My agent Ivan Mulcahy, whose calm head stilled choppy waters with Celtic charm.

My greatest debt, as ever, is to my wife Sue, who wielded chopsticks, slurped noodles, gave me space and played full-time mum to Tom and Ruby for more months than she should have.

Inside cover front: People waiting outside wagamama Bridge Street, Sydney, 2003. © Hamilton Lund
Inside cover back: The lunchtime queue outside the first ever wagamama in London's Bloomsbury, 1992. © Philip Sayer